Early Childhood Education and Development in Indonesia

A WORLD BANK STUDY

Early Childhood Education and Development in Indonesia

An Assessment of Policies Using SABER

Amina Denboba, Amer Hasan, and Quentin Wodon, Editors

WORLD BANK GROUP

ISBN (paper): 978-1-4648-0646-9
ISBN (electronic): 978-1-4648-0651-3
DOI: 10.1596/978-1-4648-0646-9

Cover photo: © Hafid Alatas. Used with permission; further permission required for reuse.
Cover design: Debra Naylor, Naylor Design, Inc.

Library of Congress Cataloging-in-Publication Data has been requested

Contents

Boxes

Figures

Tables

Acknowledgments

This research received generous support from the Dutch Education Support Program trust fund (TF057272), the SABER umbrella trust fund managed by the Education Global Practice at the World Bank, and the Global Partnership for Education. The opinions expressed in the study are those of the individual authors only and need not represent those of the World Bank, its Executive Directors, or the countries they represent. This study benefited from substantial guidance from the Education Global Practice management, including Luis Benveniste (Practice Manager), Harry Patrinos (Practice Manager), Amit Dar (Director), and Claudia Costin (Senior Director).

The team expresses their sincere gratitude to the government of Indonesia for its support:

- Nina Sardjunani, Deputy of Human Resource and Culture, Ministry of National Development Planning
- Subandi, Director of Education, Ministry of National Development Planning
- Siswanto Roesyidi, Deputy of People's Welfare, Secretary of Cabinet
- Nugaan Yulia Wardhani Siregar, Director of Teacher and Education Personnel for Early Childhood Education and Development, Ministry of Education and Culture
- Burhanuddin, Director of Toddler-Family Group and Children, National Population and Family Planning Agency
- Sukiman, Head of Sub-Directorate Program and Evaluation, Ministry of Education and Culture
- Theresia Sandra Dyah Ratih, Head of Sub-Directorate Immunization, Ministry of Health
- Puti Chairida Anwar, Head of Sub-Directorate Children Social Welfare, Ministry of Social Affairs
- Dwinita Yoenus, Head of Learning Program, Sub-Directorate Student and Learning, Ministry of Education and Culture
- Sudadi, Head of Section Program, Sub-Directorate Program and Evaluation, Ministry of Education and Culture

- Ina Nurohmah, Directorate General of Early Childhood Education and Development, Ministry of Education and Culture
- Valentinus Sudarjanto, Directorate General of Village Community Empowerment, Ministry of Home Affairs.

The team also acknowledges the local governments of Sukabumi District, Pacitan District, Sumbawa District, Kapuas District, and Manggarai Timur District for their support and feedback during the district-level study:

- District Planning and Development Agency
- District Education Office
- District Health Office
- District Social Affairs
- District Community Empowerment and Village Governance
- District Religious Affairs Office
- Family Planning and Women Empowerment Agency.

About the Contributors

Lindsay Adams has been working on social development issues for 10 years. She is currently a consultant at the World Bank and focuses on early childhood development. She works in the World Bank's Global Education and Knowledge Group in the Education Global Practice and has authored a number of Systems Approach for Better Education Results-Early Childhood Development (SABER-ECD) reports. Lindsay contributed to an evaluation of the Global Partnership for Education conducted by Results for Development. Prior to working on ECD, she worked at foundations promoting social development and human rights in the Middle East.

Amina Denboba is an early childhood development specialist with the Education Global Practice of the World Bank, with several years of experience in international development. Prior to that she worked at the American Institutes for Research where she managed School Health and Nutrition programs in Sub-Saharan Africa through operational and technical support to in-country School Health and Nutrition program implementers. Her experience covers research, policy dialogue, project design and implementation, and program management. She is an author of *Stepping Up Early Childhood Development: Investing in Young Children for High Returns* (2014) and several publications under the World Bank flagship program SABER. She holds an MA in international economics from the University of Pierre Mendes France in Grenoble, France, and a BA in economics and applied management from the University of Jean Moulin in Lyon, France.

Titie Hadiyati has been working in the field of early childhood education and development (ECED) since 1998. She has worked closely with colleagues in the Directorate in implementing the ECD-1 and ECED programs under the existing and newly established regulations on early childhood education. Her area of expertise includes community-based ECED service provision, among others. As a project management specialist, she was co-task team leader for the Early Childhood Education and Development Project and one of the task team leaders for the Regional Development Project at the World Bank in Indonesia.

Djoko Hartono is a monitoring and evaluation (M&E) specialist with more than 10 years of experience in directly managing M&E of various development projects in Indonesia. He holds a PhD in demography from Australia National University. He joined the World Bank's Jakarta Office in 2006 as an M&E specialist in education programs. He currently works as an M&E specialist in the World Bank's PNPM Generasi program. Before joining the World Bank, he was a researcher at the Indonesia Institute of Sciences (LIPI) with a major focus on policy research in the area of population and human development. Since 2012, he has been a research associate for a LIPI research project on maternal and child health among disadvantaged migrants residing in urban slums in several cities in Indonesia.

Amer Hasan is an economist with the Education Global Practice of the World Bank. He is a team leader for the impact evaluation of the Indonesia Early Childhood Education and Development project, a government program to expand access to pre school services in rural areas. His current work focuses on Indonesia and China and ranges from early childhood education to technical and vocational education and training. He holds a PhD and a master's degree in public policy from the University of Chicago as well as a BA in history from Yale University.

Janice Heejin Kim has been working on education and social development issues for seven years. She is currently a consultant at the Global Education and Knowledge Group in the Education Global Practice at the World Bank, focusing on early childhood development. Before joining the Bank, she worked at the Organization for Economic Cooperation and Development (OECD) and has authored the *Starting Strong III—A Quality Toolbox for Early Childhood Education and Care* and a number of country reports on early childhood education system in OECD countries.

Mayla Safuro Lestari Putri received a degree in economics from Universitas Gadjah Mada. She currently works as research analyst at the World Bank for early childhood education and development programs in Indonesia. Her expertise is in unified database management, survey development, and policy mapping. In collaboration with ministerial and district officers, she was one of two principal interviewers conducting SABER-ECD to understand the policy environment around early childhood education and development in Indonesia. Her research interests include survey and population analysis of education, health, and social welfare problems using longitudinal data such as the National Socioeconomic Survey (*Survei Sosial Ekonomi Nasional*, SUSENAS) and the Indonesian Family Life Survey.

Rosfita Roesli is a senior education specialist with the Education Global Practice based in the World Bank's Jakarta Office. She was one of the task team leaders of the Indonesia Early Childhood Education and Development Project. She holds a master of arts degree in development studies from the University of Leeds, United Kingdom.

Rebecca Sayre is an early childhood development and education specialist with professional experience in Africa, Latin America, and the United States. She previously served as a core team member of the World Bank's SABER-ECD initiative in Washington, DC. She has co-authored numerous publications, including *Investing in Early Childhood Development: Review of the World Bank's Recent Experience* (2014) and *Stepping Up Early Childhood Development: Investing in Young Children for High Returns* (2014). She has consulted for the Brookings Center for Universal Education, Results for Development Institute, UNICEF, and Centro de Investigación y Docencia Económica. Rebecca's two-year position as a Peace Corps volunteer in rural Peru sparked her personal and professional commitment to early childhood development in low-resource settings. Rebecca holds a BA in psychology, Spanish, and global and public health from the University of Virginia and an EdM in international education policy from the Harvard Graduate School of Education.

Quentin Wodon is a lead economist for education at the World Bank. Previously, he managed the World Bank unit on values and development, served as the lead poverty specialist for Africa, and as an economist/senior economist for Latin America. Before joining the World Bank, he was an assistant brand manager with Procter & Gamble, a volunteer corps member with the International Movement ATD Fourth World, and a tenured professor at the University of Namur. He has also taught at American University and Georgetown University. Quentin holds PhDs in economics and theology and religious studies. He has authored or coauthored more than 450 publications and serves on various advisory boards, professional association boards, and as associate editor for journals. He is actively involved with Rotary International and in pro bono consulting for nonprofits.

Executive Summary

Introduction

Since the early 2000s, Indonesia has taken a number of steps to prioritize early childhood development (ECD)—ranging from its inclusion of ECD in the National Education System Law No. 20 in 2003 to a Presidential Declaration on Holistic and Integrated ECD and the launch of the country's first-ever ECD Census in 2011. These policy milestones have occurred in parallel with sustained progress on outcomes included in the Millennium Development Goals, for issues including child malnutrition, child mortality, and universal basic education. Additional progress could be achieved by strengthening ECD policies further. This report presents findings from an assessment of ECD policies and programs in Indonesia using two World Bank tools: the ECD module of the Systems Approach for Better Education Results (SABER) and the Stepping Up ECD guide on essential interventions for investing in young children. Results from the application of both tools to Indonesia are used to suggest a number of policy options to strengthen the Indonesian ECD system that policy makers and ECD practitioners should consider.

Assessment of ECD Policies

The assessment of ECD policies at the national and district level is based on the SABER-ECD diagnostic tool which is structured around three policy goals: establishing an enabling environment, implementing widely, and monitoring and assuring quality. For each policy goal, three policy levers are analyzed through which decision makers can strengthen ECD (figure ES.1).

The quality of policies at the level of goals or levers is rated on a four-point scale (latent, emerging, established, and advanced). At the national level, ratings obtained for Indonesia tend to be higher than those obtained by other countries for six of the policy levers (table ES.1 and figure ES.2), but they are below average for program coverage, equity, and compliance with standards.

- *Establishing an enabling environment (established rating)*: Indonesia has enacted many key laws to ensure young children's well-being. The Holistic and Integrated ECD Policy is an important step in ensuring coordination as the

country tries to expand access to and quality of essential ECD services. However, funding for the sector may be insufficient.

- *Implementing widely (emerging rating)*: The scope of ECD programs in Indonesia
  is generally broad, but could be expanded, particularly in parenting, preschool
  education and nutrition. Coverage rates for some services need improvement.
  Childhood malnutrition rates are high. Vast disparities in services and outcomes
  exist between wealthier and poorer families, as well as between families living
  in urban and rural locations. Children with special needs are unlikely to have
  access to appropriate services, despite policy goals to provide inclusive services.
- *Monitoring and assuring quality (emerging rating)*: Indonesia collects a wide variety
  of administrative and survey data. The government has established many important ECD delivery and infrastructure standards. Some teachers do not meet qualifications, and only a small percentage of early childhood centers are accredited.

Figure ES.1   Three Core Early Childhood Development Policy Goals

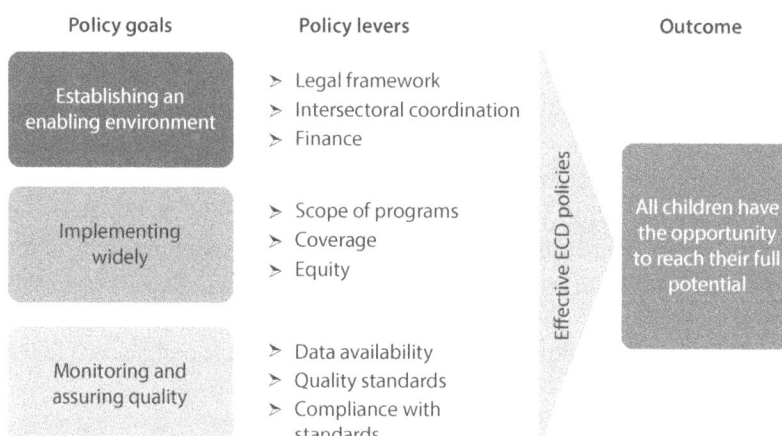

Source: Neuman and Devercelli 2013.

Table ES.1   Comparative Performance of Indonesia for SABER-ECD Goals and Levers

	Goal 1: Enabling environment	Goal 2: Implementing widely	Goal 3: Ensuring quality	Lever 1: Legal framework	Lever 2: Coordination mechanism	Lever 3: Finance
Indonesia	3	2	2.5	3	3	3
Average	2.1	2.4	2.1	2.4	1.9	2.1
	Lever 4: Scope of programs	Lever 5: Coverage of programs	Lever 6: Equity in coverage	Lever 7: Data availability	Lever 8: Quality standards	Lever 9: Compliance with standards
Indonesia	3	2	2	3	2.9	1.7
Average	2.5	2.6	2.3	2.1	2.5	1.6

Source: World Bank SABER-ECD Survey.
Note: Each number indicates the level of development in ECD policy at the national level. "1" = latent, "2" = emerging, "3" = established, and
"4" = advanced. Average indicates the average rating of 28 countries that have participated in the SABER-ECD Survey. SABER-ECD =
Systems Approach for Better Education Results-Early Childhood Development.

Figure ES.2 SABER-ECD Ratings for Indonesia and Other Countries

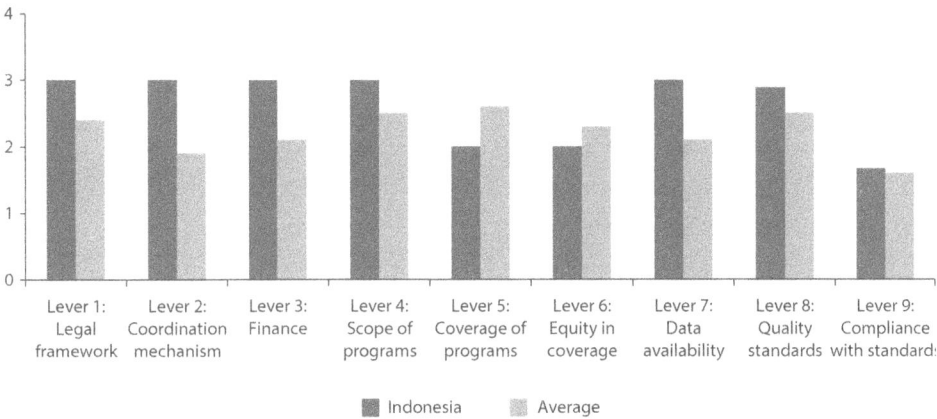

Source: Based on data in table ES.1.

The SABER-ECD module was also piloted in five districts, given that the implementation of ECD policies has been decentralized at that level. Results from the tool reveal substantial differences across districts in the quality of ECD policies and programs. As expected, on average, across policy goals and levers, districts located in richer provinces tend to perform better than districts located in poorer provinces, but not on all dimensions. District-level strategies and institutional anchors to coordinate service delivery across sectors are not always set up. While some districts have mandated universal coverage for some interventions, others have not. Many programs have limited coverage. To increase coverage among vulnerable groups, higher budget allocations are required. The criteria for such allocations need to be refined. Data collection and analysis also needs to be improved, as does the ability to enforce compliance with standards to ensure quality.

Coverage of Essential ECD Interventions

When compared to other countries where the SABER-ECD module has been applied, Indonesia tends to perform less well in three areas: program coverage, equity, and compliance with standards. An analysis of the coverage of 25 essential ECD interventions confirms areas with low coverage, as well as major disparities between provinces. The 25 interventions are listed in figure ES.3 according to the type of intervention considered and the sector that implements them.

Data on the coverage of the interventions are provided in figure ES.4. Some services have high coverage across provinces (antenatal care, entry in primary school, and births attended by skilled personnel), but others have low coverage (enrollment in preprimary education, secondary school completion for mothers, and deworming medication). In addition, differences in coverage between

Figure ES.3   Essential Early Childhood Development Interventions

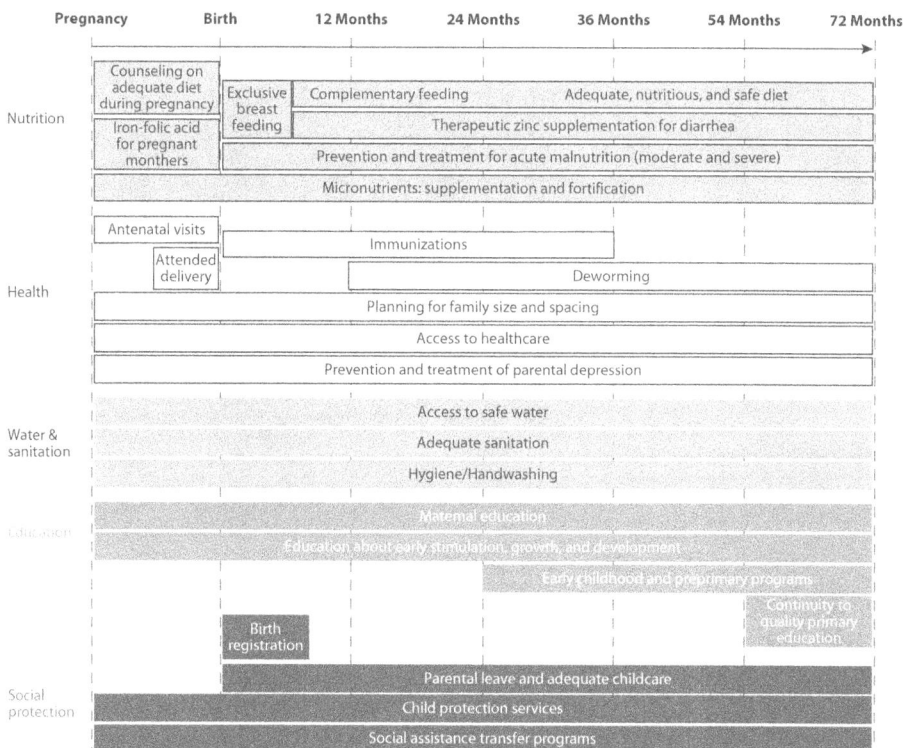

Pregnancy	Birth	12 Months	24 Months	36 Months	54 Months	72 Months

Nutrition
- Counseling on adequate diet during pregnancy
- Iron-folic acid for pregnant monthers
- Exclusive breast feeding
- Complementary feeding
- Adequate, nutritious, and safe diet
- Therapeutic zinc supplementation for diarrhea
- Prevention and treatment for acute malnutrition (moderate and severe)
- Micronutrients: supplementation and fortification

Health
- Antenatal visits
- Attended delivery
- Immunizations
- Deworming
- Planning for family size and spacing
- Access to healthcare
- Prevention and treatment of parental depression

Water & sanitation
- Access to safe water
- Adequate sanitation
- Hygiene/Handwashing

Education
- Maternal education
- Education about early stimulation, growth, and development
- Early childhood and preprimary programs
- Continuity to quality primary education

Social protection
- Birth registration
- Parental leave and adequate childcare
- Child protection services
- Social assistance transfer programs

Source: Denboba et al. 2014.

provinces are very large, often at 40–50 percentage points as shown in figure ES.4. In that figure, the diamond represents the national coverage level, and the bar represents the gap between the lowest and highest coverage rate at the level of provinces. When looking at trends over time, there have been gains in coverage between 2002 and 2012, but again with large differences between provinces, as well as differences in gains depending on the interventions.

Policy Options

On the basis of the aforementioned diagnostic, a number of policy options could be considered at both the national and district levels to strengthen ECD policies and programs. While some of these options can be put into place fairly quickly, others, also critically important, will take more time. Therefore, as shown in table ES.2, policy options are classified into short- and medium-term options at the national level (N), district level (D), or both (N&D).

Figure ES.4 Coverage of Essential Early Childhood Development Interventions, 2012

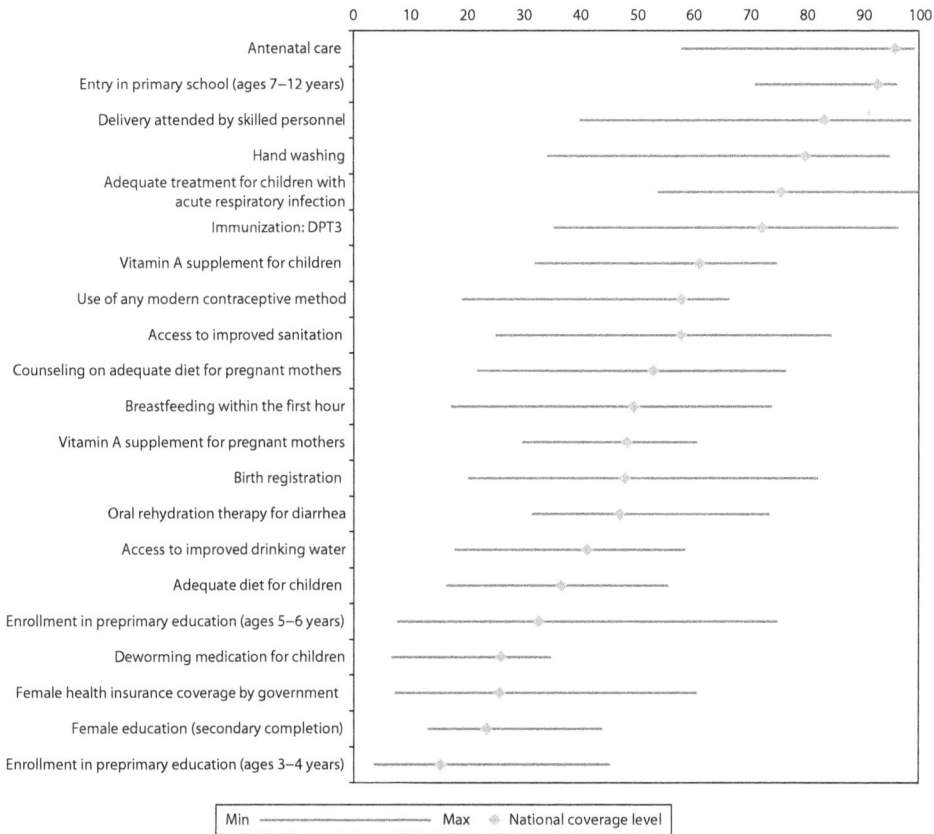

	0	10	20	30	40	50	60	70	80	90	100

Antenatal care
Entry in primary school (ages 7–12 years)
Delivery attended by skilled personnel
Hand washing
Adequate treatment for children with acute respiratory infection
Immunization: DPT3
Vitamin A supplement for children
Use of any modern contraceptive method
Access to improved sanitation
Counseling on adequate diet for pregnant mothers
Breastfeeding within the first hour
Vitamin A supplement for pregnant mothers
Birth registration
Oral rehydration therapy for diarrhea
Access to improved drinking water
Adequate diet for children
Enrollment in preprimary education (ages 5–6 years)
Deworming medication for children
Female health insurance coverage by government
Female education (secondary completion)
Enrollment in preprimary education (ages 3–4 years)

Min ——————— Max   ◆ National coverage level

Source: 2012 IDHS and SUSENAS surveys.
Note: DPT = diphtheria, pertussis, and tetanus.

Early Childhood Education and Development in Indonesia • http://dx.doi.org/10.1596/978-1-4648-0646-9

Table ES.2 Policy Options to Strengthen ECD in Indonesia

Short term (within 2 years)	Level	Medium term (3–5 years)	Level
1. Establishing an enabling environment			
Establish mechanisms for coordination between state and nonstate actors.	N&D	Mandate attendance in preprimary education for children ages 3–6 years old.	N
Develop formulas for ECD budget allocations to improve targeting and transparency.	N&D	Raise awareness among districts on the HI- ECD policy.	N
Track ECD expenditures multisectorally, particularly in child and social protection sectors.	N&D	Extend maternity and paternity leave to allow greater flexibility in workforce participation and proper caregiving for infants.	N
Appoint a district-level institutional anchor or joint secretariat to coordinate ECD service delivery across sectors.	D	Increase funding for early childhood care and education to ensure quality and access.	N&D
Improve collaboration between district offices to build HI ECD systems beyond education, including the health, nutrition, child and social protection sectors.	D	Increase budget allocations to expand implementation of HI-ECD programs.	D
Strengthen effective communication between district offices through annual HI-ECD development planning.	D		
2. Implementing widely			
Use Village Law No. 6/2014 to encourage village governments to provide quality early childhood services through the village budget (*Anggaran Dana Desa*).	N&D	Expand coverage of essential programs particularly those targeting disadvantaged children from poor families, rural or border areas and children with special needs. For example, initiate fee-free birth registration and provide low-cost services for disadvantaged children.	N&D
Incentivize villages to experiment with integrative services and encourage community participation in funding and service provision decisions.	N&D		
Improve childhood immunizations requirement.	N	Ensure all pregnant women are covered in the new *Jaminan Kesehatan Nasional* insurance scheme. Maternal depression screening and treatment could help both mothers and children.	N
3. Monitoring and assuring quality			
Track access to ECD programs and monitor child-level outcomes to identify children in need of additional support, particularly among vulnerable groups.	N&D	Establish a one-source-data collection system for consistent use among district offices to help in the mapping of children and their needs at the district level.	D
Broaden access and enhance quality of in-service training (*Diklat Berjenjang*) and professional development opportunities for early child-hood educators, particularly in nonformal centers. Fee-free in-service training could be considered.	N&D	Monitor individual child development outcomes as part of an early detection program (*Stimulasi dan Intervensi Dini Tumbuh Kembang*).	N&D

table continues next page

Table ES.2 Policy Options to Strengthen ECD in Indonesia (continued)

Short term (within 2 years)	Level	Medium term (3–5 years)	Level
Broaden training for village health workers (cadres and village midwives) to cover the links between early health and cognitive development.	N&D	Increase minimum hours of attendance at centers to increase dosage.	N
		Improve compliance with quality standards by enforcing established accreditation procedures for facilities	D
		Develop a stronger role for ECD supervisors in quality assurance.	D

Note: N = national; D = district; N&D = both national and district; ECD = early childhood development; HI-ECD = Holistic Integrated-Early Childhood Development.

Abbreviations

ADD	*Anggaran Dana Desa*
APBD	*Anggaran Pendapatan dan Belanja Daerah* (Provincial or District Government Budget)
BSNP	*Badan Standar Nasional Pendidikan* (National Education Standards Board)
DAU	*Dana Alokasi Umum* (General Allocation Fund)
DHS	Demographic and Health Survey
DPT	diphtheria, pertussis, and tetanus
ECC	Early Childhood Commission
ECCE	early childhood care and education
ECD	early childhood development
ECE	early childhood education
ECED	early childhood education and development
GoI	government of Indonesia
HI-ECD	Holistic Integrated-Early Childhood Development
HIV	human immunodeficiency virus
IDR	Indonesian rupiah
JKN	*Jaminan Kesehatan Nasional* (national health insurance program)
MICS	Multiple Indicator Cluster Survey
PNPM	*Program Nasional Pemberdayaan Masyarakat* (National Program for Community Empowerment)
PNS	*Pegawai Negeri Sipil* (civil service)
PPP	purchasing power parity
SABER	Systems Approach for Better Education Results
UN	United Nations
UNAIDS	United Nations Programme on HIV and AIDS
UNESCO	United Nations Educational, Scientific and Cultural Organization
UNICEF	United Nations Children's Fund
WHO	World Health Organization

CHAPTER 1

Overview

Amina Denboba, Amer Hasan, and Quentin Wodon

Introduction

Investing in children in their early years represents a unique window of opportunity to improve individual, community, and societal outcomes. For poverty reduction and shared prosperity, investments in early childhood development (ECD) or early childhood education and development (ECED), to use the terminology used in Indonesia, are among the best investments that countries can make. When young children and their families have access to essential services in education, health, nutrition, sanitation, social protection, and water, they are afforded the opportunity to learn and lead healthy and productive lives. The returns to ECD interventions have been shown to be often larger than the returns for interventions later in life. Conversely, failing to invest early in life can lead to irreversible damage for the future.

Indonesia has benefitted from robust economic growth over the last decade. Nevertheless, more than 27 million people still live in poverty (12.2 percent of the population), and a larger number remain vulnerable. There are very large wealth disparities between the various islands that lead to differences in development outcomes, including for young children. The fact that Indonesia has the fourth largest population in the world with many different ethnic and linguistic groups also contributes to disparities in development outcomes within the country.

Since the early 2000s, Indonesia has taken a number of decisive steps to prioritize early childhood development—ranging from the inclusion of ECD in the National Education System Law No. 20 in 2003 to a Presidential Declaration on Holistic and Integrated Early Childhood Development to the launch of the country's first ever ECD Census in 2011. Box 1.1 presents some of the key milestones of progress in ECED that Indonesia has achieved. These policy milestones have occurred in parallel with sustained progress towards many of the Millennium Development Goals. For example, Indonesia has already met and surpassed projected reductions in the number of underweight children younger than five years of age to less than 18 percent and is on track to meeting its targets for reducing overall child mortality and the targets for achieving universal basic education.

Box 1.1   Indonesia and Milestones of Progress in ECED

For more than a decade, the government of Indonesia has implemented policies and programs that prioritize the early years. The first critical step was taken in 2001, when a new directorate dedicated to early childhood was established within the Ministry of Education and Culture. Its early advocacy within and beyond the government influenced policy development, put additional resources into community ECED services, and created strategies to raise Indonesian awareness about the importance of the early years. The United Nations Children's Fund (UNICEF) initiated integrated health service clinics for mothers and children (*Taman Posyandus*) as part of their Smart Toddler program (*Balita Cerdas*), one component of the government's initiatives to support early childhood.

The second critical step was taken when early childhood education was included in a succession of key policy documents: the National Education System Law No. 20 in 2003 and the Ministry of Education and Culture's Strategic Plan (*Rencana Strategis* or RENSTRA) in 2004.

In the context of these institutional and policy changes, a pilot project covering 12 districts, which had begun under the purview of the Directorate of Community Education, was transferred to the supervision of the newly formed Directorate of Early Childhood Education. The pilot project established new ECED services in poor villages. It previewed and provided key lessons that were subsequently incorporated into a larger-scale project initiated in 2006 covering 3,000 villages in 50 districts.

More recently, the need to consider ECED services holistically, across sectors and developmental domains, was recognized through the government's issuance of an ambitious policy strategy and accompanying guidelines in 2008. The development of national standards for ECED by the National Education Standards Board (BSNP) in 2009 situated early childhood education as the foundation of the country's education system.

A lingering barrier to coordinated ECED service provision was removed when the "formal" and "nonformal" directorates were merged into one unit in 2010 with responsibility for all ECED activities. Finally, the initiation of ECED censuses since 2011 has begun to provide researchers and policy makers with essential data and should continue to inform future ECED decisions.

Source: Hasan, Hyson, and Chang 2013.

Yet, according to 2010 census data, the number of children under six years of age is almost 32 million, making the needs for service delivery massive.

This study provides an assessment of ECD policies and programs in Indonesia based on the World Bank's Systems Approach for Better Education Results (SABER). Developed by the Education Global Practice, SABER provides a set of diagnostic tools to assess country policies in a number of areas including ECD. The SABER-ECD tool employs a diagnostic framework structured around three policy goals: establishing an enabling environment, implementing widely, and monitoring and assuring quality. For each goal, three policy levers are analyzed, ranging from the legal framework for ECD services to the extent to which service providers such as care centers or preschools comply with national standards (Neuman and Devercelli 2013). Country policies are assessed along each of these dimensions. The SABER-ECD tool to a large extent focuses on policy intent, but as its name indicates, the second policy goal in the ECD module is about implementation. To this end, the analysis is complemented by a more detailed analysis of the coverage of essential interventions at the provincial level.

The study relies on administrative and household survey data in order to provide a diagnostic of policies and programs related to ECD in Indonesia. Administrative data are used to assess ECD policies and programs at the national and district levels. The study consists of five chapters:

- Chapter 2 applies the SABER-ECD framework at the national level. Strengthening ECD policies can be viewed as a continuum; for each policy goal and corresponding policy levers, a policy classification rubric comprising a range of indicators and subindicators is used to calculate levels of policy development. For each subindicator, a score of latent (1 point), emerging (2 points), established (3 points), or advanced (4 points) is allotted. Then, the indicator score is calculated from the average of subindicators. Finally, the level of policy development for each policy lever is calculated from the average of the indicator scores. The policy lever scores are then averaged to form a score for each policy goal.

- Building on the application of the SABER-ECD framework in Indonesia, both at the national and district levels, chapter 3 focuses on measuring in a more comprehensive way the coverage of essential ECD interventions nationally and at the provincial level. The list of interventions is based on a framework identifying 25 key programs for young children and their families. For 19 of 25 interventions, information is available in the nationally representative household surveys, especially from the 2002, 2007, and 2012 Demographic and Health Surveys (DHS), and the 2007 and 2012 SUSENAS surveys in the case of interventions for the preschool package.

- Given the decentralization of many ECD policies and programs at the district level, chapter 4 provides results from the application of the SABER-ECD framework to five districts. While this represents only about 1 percent of all districts, the results are interesting to showcase differences in policies and programs between districts. As expected, on average across policy goals and corresponding policy levers, districts located in richer provinces tend to perform better than districts located in poorer provinces, but not on all dimensions.

- Chapter 5 compares the SABER-ECD ratings obtained for Indonesia with the ratings for other countries (in total, the tool has been implemented in about 28 countries so far). The chapter also provides illustrations of selected examples of best practice policies for all three policy goals and various dimensions from around the world that could potentially provide inspiration for improved policy development in Indonesia.

CHAPTER 2

National SABER-ECD Assessment for Indonesia

Lindsay Adams, Amina Denboba, Titie Hadiyati, Djoko Hartono,
Amer Hasan, Janice Heejin Kim, Rosfita Roesli, Mayla Safuro,
and Quentin Wodon

Abstract

The Systems Approach for Better Education Results (SABER) produces comparative data and knowledge on education policies and institutions, with the aim of helping countries strengthen their education systems. In the case of Early Childhood Development (ECD—this will be the acronym used in this study even though the acronym used in Indonesia is *early childhood education and development*, or ECED), the focus is on early learning, health, nutrition, as well as social and child protection policies. SABER-ECD evaluates the quality of policies against evidence-based global standards, using a diagnostic tool and detailed policy data collected from administrative sources and in-depth key informant interviews. This chapter applies the SABER-ECD framework to Indonesia.

Introduction

As noted by Denboba et al. (2014), investing in children in their early years represents a unique window of opportunity to improve individual, community, and societal outcomes. For poverty reduction and shared prosperity, investments in early childhood development (ECD) are among the best investments that countries can make. When young children and their families have access to essential services in education, health, nutrition, sanitation, social protection, and water, they are afforded the opportunity to learn and lead healthy and productive lives. The returns to ECD interventions have been shown to be often larger than the returns for interventions later in life. Conversely, failing to invest early in life can lead to irreversible damage for the future. Unfortunately, most countries today fall short in their ECD investments.

Table 2.1 considers how Indonesia is investing in ECD and provides a snapshot of selected ECD outcome indicators in the country, with a comparison with selected other countries. The focus is on infant mortality, child mortality, stunting,

Table 2.1 Snapshot of Early Childhood Development Indicators in Indonesia with Regional Comparison

	Indonesia	China	India	Philippines	Vietnam
Infant mortality (deaths per 1,000 live births, 2012)	26	12	44	24	18
Below -5 mortality (deaths per 1,000 live births, 2012)	31	14	56	30	23
Moderate and severe stunting (below 5, 2008–12) (%)	36	10	48	32	23
Gross preprimary enrollment rate[a] (5–6 years, 2011) (%)	46	62	58	—	72
Birth registration 2005–12 (%)	67	—	41	90	95

Source: UNICEF 2012.
Note: — = not available.
a. For gross preprimary enrollment rate, this chapter used data from the UNICEF–Multiple Indicator Cluster Survey. Chapters 1 and 3 used net preprimary enrollment rate data from the SUSENAS 2003–13.

the enrollment rate in preschools, and the rate of birth registration. The data for Indonesia are provided circa 2012 using a United Nations Children's Fund (UNICEF) database. Among the five countries in the table (China, India, Indonesia, the Philippines, and Vietnam), Indonesia tends to be second to last or last for all indicators, suggesting scope for improvement. To foster such improvements, the central government of Indonesia (GoI) issued a Holistic Integrated-Early Childhood Development policy (HI-ECD policy). The policy aims to provide comprehensive and integrated ECD services to all children from birth to age six years. But while the policy lays out foundations for a strong ECD system, issues remain around coverage, equity, and quality of the services provided. Administratively, the country is organized into 33 provinces and a special administrative region. Decentralization has been implemented since 2001, leading to a substantial degree of autonomy for subnational administrative units, including districts in the case of ECD programs and policies targeting young children. Box 2.1 provides an overview of the decentralized education system in Indonesia. The challenge of implementation is substantial, in part because of the size of the country. According to 2010 census data, the number of children younger than six years of age is at almost 32 million, making the needs for service delivery massive.

This chapter provides the results of the application of the SABER-ECD diagnostic tool to Indonesia at the national level (chapter 4 considers the application of the tool at the district level). The structure of the chapter is as follows. This chapter describes the SABER-ECD framework. The next three chapters provide the results of the assessment including policy options to be considered for improved policy dialogue to strengthen each policy lever assessed. As is the case for other SABER modules, the SABER-ECD module is to a large extent focused on policy intent, but as its name indicates, the second policy goal in the ECD module is about implementation. A more detailed analysis will be required to make tailored and context specific policy recommendations moving forward. A conclusion follows.

Box 2.1 How the Education System Is Financed and Managed in Indonesia's Decentralized Setup

The education system in Indonesia is a very large, highly decentralized system, with over 500 district governments playing a strong role in its management. While many ministries register spending on education in their budgets, the Ministry of Education and Culture and the Ministry of Religious Affairs are responsible for setting policies and managing the system. Under both ministries, public and private provision coexist and receive public support in the form of civil service teachers (at all levels) and direct school grants (in basic education). While the nine years of basic education (primary and junior secondary) are compulsory and heavily subsidized, household contributions are high in early childhood education services. This is partly because of widespread private provision of kindergartens and limited public support for preschool.

Both central and district governments are responsible for developing and managing the teaching force. Other central government agencies remain in charge of setting pay rates for civil servants and transferring district government budgets.

The funding system for the education sector is complex, involving multiple sources and transfers across various levels of government. Despite efforts to simplify budgets, schools still receive funds from an array of budget sources: some come directly from the central government and some from local governments (mainly districts).

Central government transfers are the main source of revenue for district government budgets (APBD). The main transfer to subnational governments is the DAU block grant, which provides funding for the salaries of district civil servants, including civil service (PNS) teachers. District and provincial governments also receive funds from different transfer mechanisms, each with specific associated incentives.

A constitutional amendment passed in 2002 establishes that at least 20 percent of the total state budget has to be spent on education. Both central and local government budgets are subject to the rule, which includes budget revisions. This rigidity creates significant distortions in decision making.

Figure B2.1.1 Financing Responsibilities under Decentralized Education Management

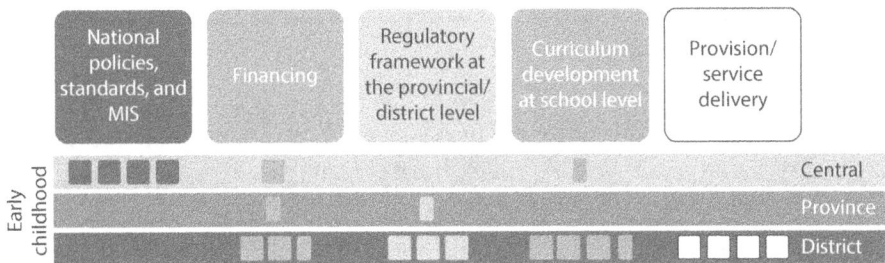

Note: Boxes indicate relative role of each level in the activity indicated in the column. Each box represents 25 percent. MIS = management information system.

While education financing remains a shared responsibility between all levels of government, the bulk of funds for pretertiary education are provided by district governments. In 2001, the responsibility for many aspects of basic education was devolved to local

box continues next page

Box 2.1 How the Education System Is Financed and Managed in Indonesia's Decentralized Setup *(continued)*

Figure B2.1.2 Composition of Public Education Spending, 2009

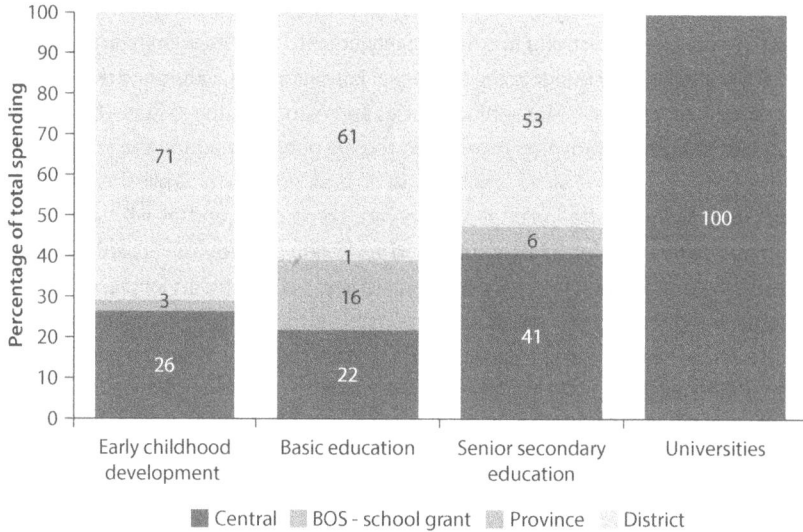

Source: World Bank 2013.
Note: Financing responsibilities in the figure reflect the main responsibilities under the education program assigned to a specific level of government. BOS = *Biaya Operasi Sekolah* (School Operation Fund).

governments. Decentralization reforms were expected to lead to significant improvements in education outcomes by bringing decision making closer to the parents and students that are directly affected. In this way, decisions on the best way to deliver education services would be increasingly responsive to local needs and more aligned with the specific characteristics of each district. Decentralization was also expected to lead to greater innovation and experimentation in service delivery with the potential for successful reforms to be replicated across local governments. In 2009, approximately 71 percent of all public education spending on ECED was provided by district governments (figure B2.1.2).

SABER-ECD Framework

SABER-ECD collects, analyzes, and disseminates comprehensive information on ECD policies around the world. In each participating country, extensive multi-sectoral information is collected on ECD policies and programs through a desk review of available government documents, data and literature, and interviews with a range of ECD stakeholders, including government officials, service providers, civil society, development partners, and scholars.

The SABER-ECD framework aims to provide a holistic and integrated assessment of how the overall policy environment in a country affects young children's development. The tool identifies three core policy goals that countries should address to ensure optimal ECD outcomes: (1) establishing an enabling environment, (2) implementing widely, and (3) monitoring and assuring quality. Improving

ECD requires an integrated approach to address all three goals. As described in figure 2.1, for each policy goal, a series of policy levers are identified, through which decision makers can strengthen ECD. Strengthening ECD policies can be viewed as a continuum; as described in table 2.2, countries can range from a latent

Figure 2.1 Three Core ECD Policy Goals

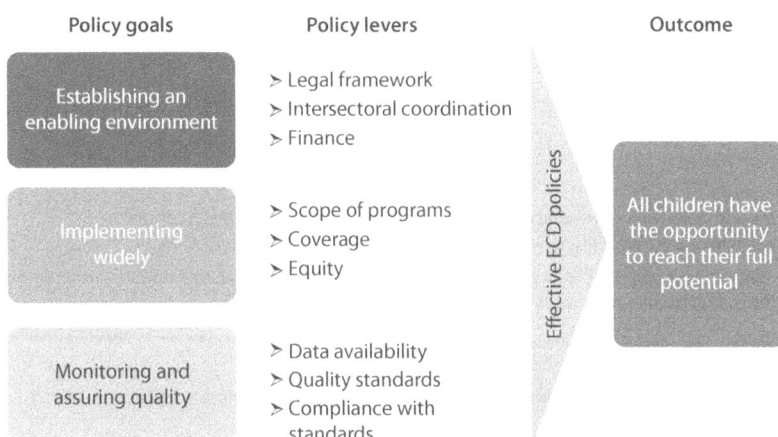

Policy goals	Policy levers		Outcome
Establishing an enabling environment	➤ Legal framework ➤ Intersectoral coordination ➤ Finance		
Implementing widely	➤ Scope of programs ➤ Coverage ➤ Equity	Effective ECD policies	All children have the opportunity to reach their full potential
Monitoring and assuring quality	➤ Data availability ➤ Quality standards ➤ Compliance with standards		

Source: Neuman and Devercelli 2013.
Note: ECD = early childhood development.

Table 2.2 ECD Policy Goals and Levels of Development

	Level of development			
	Latent ●○○○	*Emerging* ●●○○	*Established* ●●●○	*Advanced* ●●●●
ECD policy goal				
Establishing an enabling environment	Nonexistent legal framework; ad-hoc financing; low intersectoral coordination.	Minimal legal framework; some programs with sustained financing; some intersectoral coordination.	Regulations in some sectors; functioning intersectoral coordination; sustained financing.	Developed legal framework; robust interinstitutional coordination; sustained financing.
Implementing widely	Low coverage; pilot programs in some sectors; high inequality in access and outcomes.	Coverage expanding but gaps remain; programs established in a few sectors; inequality in access and outcomes.	Near-universal coverage in some sectors; established programs in most sectors; low inequality in access.	Universal coverage; comprehensive strategies across sectors; integrated services for all, some tailored and targeted.
Monitoring and assuring quality	Minimal survey data available; limited standards for provision of ECD services; no enforcement.	Information on outcomes at national level; standards for services exist in some sectors; no system to monitor compliance.	Information on outcomes at national, regional and local levels; standards for services exist for most sectors; system in place to regularly monitor compliance.	Information on outcomes from national to individual levels; standards exist for all sectors; system in place to regularly monitor and enforce compliance.

Source: Neuman and Devercelli 2013.
Note: ECD = early childhood development.

Box 2.2 Checklist to Consider How Well Early Childhood Development Is Promoted at the Country Level

Health Care
– Standard health screenings for pregnant women
– Skilled attendants at delivery
– Childhood immunizations
– Well-child visits

Nutrition
– Breastfeeding promotion
– Salt iodization
– Iron fortification

Early Learning
– Parenting programs (during pregnancy, after delivery, and throughout early childhood)
– High-quality childcare for working parents
– Free preprimary school (preferably at least two years with developmentally appropriate curriculum and classrooms, and quality assurance mechanisms)

Social Protection
– Services for orphans and vulnerable children
– Policies to protect rights of children with special needs and promote their participation/access to ECD services
– Financial transfer mechanisms or income supports to reach the most vulnerable families (could include cash transfers, and social welfare)

Child Protection
– Mandated birth registration
– Job protection and breastfeeding breaks for new mothers
– Specific provisions in judicial system for young children
– Guaranteed paid parental leave of at least six months
– Domestic violence laws and enforcement
– Tracking of child abuse (especially for young children)
– Training for law enforcement officers in regards to the particular needs of young children

Source: Adapted from Neuman and Devercelli 2013.
Note: ECD = early childhood development.

to an advanced level of development within the different policy levers and goals. The assessment provided in this chapter can be used to identify how to think about policy challenges related to ECD. Box 2.2 presents an abbreviated list of interventions and policies that the SABER-ECD tool looks at in countries when assessing the level of ECD policy development. The list is not exhaustive, but is meant to provide an initial checklist to consider when thinking about policies across sectors.

Policy Goal 1: Establishing an Enabling Environment

An enabling environment is the foundation for the design and implementation of effective ECD policies (Brinkerhoff 2009; Britto, Yoshikawa, and Boller 2011; Vargas-Baron 2005). An enabling environment consists of the following:

the existence of an adequate legal and regulatory framework to support ECD; coordination within sectors and across institutions to deliver services effectively; and sufficient fiscal resources with transparent and efficient allocation mechanisms.

Policy Lever 1.1: Legal Framework (Rating: Established)

The legal framework comprises all of the laws and regulations which can affect the development of young children in a country. The laws and regulations that impact ECD are diverse because of the array of sectors that influence ECD and because of the different constituencies that ECD policy can and should target, including pregnant women, young children, parents, and caregivers. In Indonesia, national laws promote health care for pregnant women—this policy lever is rated as established, but could nevertheless be strengthened.

The new universal health care insurance system, the *Jaminan Kesehatan Nasional* (JKN), which has been recently established and is being expanded, is a step in that direction. Wealthier citizens pay premiums, and the government provides grants to cover premiums for poor individuals. Individuals must enroll, and the scheme will be rolled out over the next several years.

JKN covers individual care including promotion, preventive, curative, and rehabilitative health services with selected condition of facility. Since the JKN policy was issued in 2013, childbirth insurance scheme (*Jaminan Persalinan, Jampersal*) is no longer applied. However, all mother and child programs (*Kesehatan Ibu dan Anak*) that were previously covered in *Jampersal* are now being covered in the new scheme, for example antenatal and neonatal care, postnatal care, and institutional delivery.

Access to screening tests and health services, as well as referrals to services, is provided for free for women or mothers who voluntarily want to get tested or as suggested by medical staff. Screening for human immunodeficiency virus (HIV) in pregnant women is not required, but is recommended for women deemed at elevated risk. The government could however consider mandated screening for all pregnant women. According to United Nations Programme on HIV and AIDS (UNAIDS), approximately 610,000 Indonesians are living with HIV—a number which could include over 8,000 pregnant women in any given year.[1] Without universal testing and treatment, HIV-positive pregnant women are at risk of passing HIV to their babies. Screening would strengthen efforts to reduce HIV transmission under the Minister of Health Regulation on HIV/AIDS Prevention no. 21/2013 and Minister of Health Regulation No. 51/2013 on HIV/AIDS Prevention from Mother to Child.

Government policies and programs provide basic health care for children. The new national health insurance system covers well-child visits. According to the Act on Child Protection, the government must provide free basic health care and referral services for children from poor families. In addition, mother and child programs, such as antenatal care and growth and development monitoring, can be implemented at all health facilities, including *Posyandu*. Young children receive a mandatory course of immunizations, but the course does not include mumps, rubella, and meningitis vaccinations. The government could consider adding these immunizations to the mandatory course in order to provide the broadest possible protection for children's health.

National laws and regulations promote appropriate dietary consumption by pregnant women and young children. The Government Regulation on Exclusive Breastfeeding and a health ministry decree establish the government's support for exclusive breastfeeding until the age of six months. Mothers are guaranteed breastfeeding breaks and facilities in places of employment. Salt iodization is mandatory, as is fortification of flour with micronutrients.

Policies protect new parents and provide parents and caregivers opportunities to care for newborns and infants, but parental leave could be extended (see table 2.3). Indonesian labor laws bar employment discrimination for pregnant women and mothers, and establishes job protection. Public and private sector workers receive 90 days of paid maternity leave, starting 1.5 months before the expected delivery. Fathers receive two days of paid paternity leave. The actual coverage of these benefits is often limited by the size of the formal sector in the economy. The GoI could consider ways of extending maternity and paternity leave to promote labor participation and proper caregiving for infants. In addition, parental leave policies should be highly flexible to allow new parents provide the appropriate and timely care for their newborn. A baby's need for caregiving, breastfeeding, and nurturing are greatest in the early months of life. Finding ways to extend the coverage of flexible parental leave could improve babies' health and development outcomes, as well as the well-being of mothers, which in turn has a strong impact on their children's well-being.

Indonesia lacks a strong policy to provide free preprimary education. Currently preprimary education is not compulsory. According to the Strategic Plan and Grand Design of ECE Development 2011–25 document issued by the Directorate General of Early Child Education, the target gross enrollment rate for early childhood care and education (ECCE) in 2015 is 75 percent. The government is promoting enrollment through establishing and expanding nonformal ECCE

Table 2.3 Regional Comparison of Maternity and Paternity Leave Policies

Indonesia	China	Thailand	Vietnam
Ninety days paid maternity leave at 100 percent wage; 2 days paid paternity leave at 100 percent wage	Ninety days paid maternity leave at 100 percent wage; no national law ensuring paternity leave, although some local governments offer it	Forty-five days of paid maternity leave at 100 percent wage, up to 45 more days of unpaid leave, although some classes of workers are not entitled to any leave; no paternity leave	Four months (roughly 120 days) of maternity leave at 100 percent wage, with extensions for certain medical or working conditions; no paternity leave

Source: ILO Working Conditions Laws Database – Maternity Protection, 2012.

centers and community-based groups. Government data for 2012 suggest that 162,748 centers are operating, but of those only 10,077 are accredited (the rest, a total of 152,671 centers, are not). Among the centers, only a small minority (3,789) are public, 132,269 are private (both for profit and nonprofit), and 26,690 are community based.

Birth registration is mandatory. The Child Protection Act states that a birth certificate establishes a child's identity and is required upon birth. Birth certificates are free and are issued by the government. Eight government ministries have signed a Memorandum of Understanding to accelerate the issuance of birth certificates.

A range of policies and services promote child protection. The Ministry of Women Empowerment and Child Protection is responsible for implementing child protection laws at the national level with district authorities charged with implementation at the local level. The government promotes the reduction of family violence through various programs, including training on identification of child abuse and neglect, child abuse tracking, violence prevention through home visits, and a taskforce for domestic violence prevention. It provides protection, counseling, and legal advocacy for victims of family violence. And it trains judges, lawyers, and law enforcement officers on protecting children.

Social protection policies and services support vulnerable children and children with special needs. Several programs provide services for vulnerable children, including the Social Block Grant for Child Welfare Agencies, PKSA Balita (Children-Welfare Program for children younger than five years of age) and TAS (Children-Welfare Program). The LKSA (Child Welfare Agency) gives block grants to government and community and private organizations to provide housing to orphans and vulnerable children, including through foster care.

The Law on Social Welfare states that social welfare must be given to people with disabilities, including children with special needs, in order to ensure that

---

Box 2.3 Key Laws Governing Early Childhood Development in Indonesia

- Presidential Regulation on National Health Insurance System No. 12/2013 and its amendment on Presidential Regulation No. 111/2013
- Child Protection Act No. 23/2002 Article 44 regarding free basic health care for poor children, birth registration, and legal protections and services
- Government Regulation No. 33/2012 on exclusive breastfeeding
- Law No. 18/2012 on food, regarding fortification with micronutrients
- Law No. 13/2003 on manpower, regarding parental leave and nondiscrimination
- Presidential Decree No. 60/2013, regarding the HI-ECD Law No. 23/2004, regarding elimination of domestic violence
- Law on Social Welfare No. 11/2009, regarding social protection, housing, and special needs services.

---

their basic needs are met. The definition of disability used encompasses physical, mental, and socioemotional delays and disorders, including attention deficit hyperactivity disorder and autism. The Ministry of Women Empowerment and Child Protection is the lead agency for directing special needs services, and it has established guidelines to be used by other ministries providing services to children with special needs, including the Ministry of Education, Ministry of Health, and Ministry of Information.

On the basis of the aforementioned diagnostic, a number of policy options could be considered to strengthen the legal framework for ECD:

- Socialize the issuance of HI-ECD policy to the local level, as well as the technical guidance for its implementation. Despite having the HI-ECD policy issued, district governments still have limited information on how to implement the policy.
- Consider mandating preprimary education for children ages three to six years. Without quality preschool, many children enter primary school without the skills they need to succeed in education. Attending quality preprimary programs is associated with many lifelong benefits to individuals, as well as to the economic well-being of a country. In the near term, the GoI could consider increasing attendance in preprimary education, dependent on the development of quality preschool models.
- Consider making vaccines for mumps, rubella, and meningitis mandatory for the immunization course young children receive. This would improve children's health and reduce health care costs by decreasing the need for medical treatment.
- Encourage HIV screening of pregnant or vulnerable women, and raise awareness of HIV. Universal screening of HIV in pregnant women has the potential to prevent cases of mother-to-child-transmission. Mandatory screening recommendation is difficult to implement because many districts do not have laboratory facilities and human capacity to deliver HIV screening tests for pregnant women. Even when testing is available (which it may not be in all Indonesian health centers), many will opt not to be screened because of stigma surrounding the disease.
- Parental leave policies should be highly flexible to allow new parents to provide appropriate and timely care for their newborn. Improve maternity and paternity leave to promote labor participation and proper caregiving for infants. Also consider socializing the importance of paternity leave since most parents have limited information on this. A baby's need for caregiving, breastfeeding, and nurturing are greatest in the early months of life. Extending paternity leave and making the maternity period more flexible could improve babies' health and development outcomes, as well as the well-being of mothers (which in turn has a strong impact on their children's well-being). The current length of leave may not be adequate for parents to devote the time and energy to caregiving that is necessary for children's healthy development. Longer parental leave makes it easier for women to remain in the workforce after having children.

Policy Lever 1.2: Intersectoral Coordination (Rating: Established)

Development in early childhood is a multidimensional process (see, for example, Naudeau et al. 2011; UNESCO-OREALC 2004; and Neuman 2007). To meet children's diverse needs during the early years, government coordination is essential, both horizontally across different sectors and vertically from the local to national levels. In many countries, nonstate actors (either domestic or international) participate in ECD service delivery; for this reason, mechanisms to coordinate with nonstate actors are also essential.

The HI-ECD policy is the GoI's multisectoral ECD policy, covering education, health, nutrition, social protection, and child protection. Issued in 2013, relevant ministries and institutions are currently elaborating their work plans and budgets to implement the policy. Each fiscal year at the National Coordination Meeting, (*Musrenbang*), central government agencies, subnational and local government representatives, meet to coordinate their programs hosted by Ministry of National Development Planning (see figure 2.2). A national level task force is delegated to coordinate the HI-ECD policy. The policy was issued by the central government and gives numerous ministries and institutions various responsibilities to implement the policy.

The policy is endorsed by numerous bodies, including the National Population and Family Planning Agency, Cabinet Secretary, Coordinating Ministry of People's Welfare, Ministry of National Development Planning, Ministry of Home

Figure 2.2 Intersectoral Coordination in Indonesia

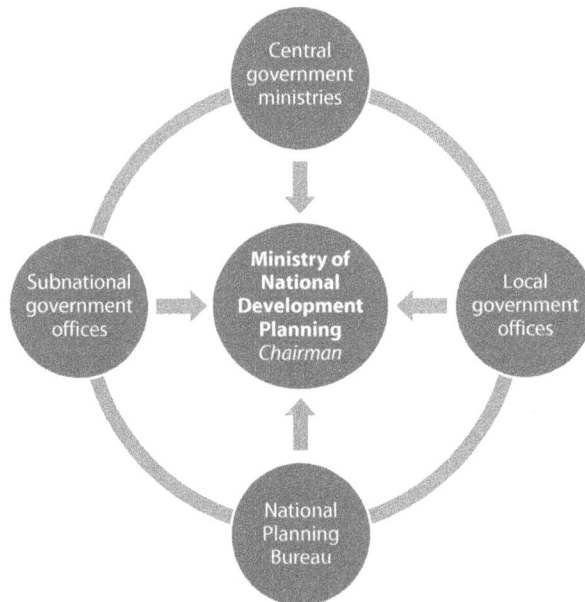

Note: Central government ministries include People's Welfare Education and Culture, Health, Women's Empowerment and Child Protection, Home Affairs, Social Affairs, Religious Affairs, National Population Affairs and Family Planning Agency, and Statistic Central Bureau.

Affairs, Ministry of Education and Culture, Ministry of Health, Ministry of Social Affairs, Ministry of Religious Affairs, and Ministry of Women Empowerment and Child Protection. The Ministry of People's Welfare (*Menko Kesra*) is the lead agency coordinating ECD efforts across ministries and institutions.

The central government is responsible for the legal framework of the policy, establishing norms, standards, procedures, and criteria; and providing technical guidance supervision, advocacy and training. The subnational/provincial government provides technical assistance, supervision, advocacy, and training. The district governments' role is to provide services, technical assistance, supervision, advocacy, training service providers, and reporting and evaluating. Coordination meetings and national and ministry-specific guidelines help ensure children receive integrated services. Service providers aim to meet regularly to coordinate service delivery. At the district level, ECD Forums and ECCE staff associations are supposed to meet at least once a month. In some districts, actors meet regularly; others do not. The Ministry of Education and Culture makes block grants to most districts in Indonesia for teacher meetings, known as ECE service cluster meetings. Some of the participants at these meetings provide integrated ECD services not limited to education. Participants share experiences and discuss issues of common concern.

The National Guidelines for HI-ECD services outline children's basic needs according to their age in health, nutrition, child protection and welfare, parenting, early stimulation, and education. Relevant ministries jointly prepared the guidelines, with support from UNICEF. Each ministry has its own guidelines based on the tasks delegated to it by Presidential Regulation. In addition, each sector has set target goals for coverage rates for services.

On the basis of this diagnostic, a number of policy options could be considered to strengthen coordination mechanisms for ECD:

- Strengthen communication between sectors through the coordination meeting held by the HI-ECD national task force. As stated in the HI-ECD policy, the national task force should hold a coordination meeting at least once every three months.
- Establish mechanisms for coordination at the national level between state and nonstate stakeholders. There do not seem to be meetings or structures for coordination between governmental and civil society organizations at the national level, although coordination of this nature seems to occur at the local level. Nonstate actors often provide many ECD services, and coordination with them may be necessary to provide children with a full range of services. Coordination can also help ensure all service providers follow standards for service delivery.

Policy Lever 1.3: Finance (Rating: Established)

While legal frameworks and intersectoral coordination are crucial to establishing an enabling environment for ECD, adequate financial investment is needed to ensure that resources are available to implement policies and achieve service provision goals. Investments in ECD can yield high public returns, but are often undersupplied without government support. Investments during the early years can yield greater returns than equivalent investments made later in a child's life cycle and can lead to long-lasting intergenerational benefits (Hanushek and Kimko 2000; Hanushek and Luque 2003; Valerio and Garcia 2012). Not only do investments in ECD generate high returns, but they can also enhance the effectiveness of other social investments and help governments address multiple priorities with single investments.

Central-level budgets use explicit criteria to determine ECD spending. In education, the GoI considers the number of children served, school construction or renovation projects, and educational materials required. Block grants to fund staff are based on the number of institutions, number of staff, and staff salaries. In the social protection and child protection sectors, the number of children covered, children's characteristics, and geographical location are used to determine allocations. In the health and nutrition sectors, ECD budget processes consider children's characteristics, geographical location, usage, historical precedent, and the number of caregiver positions. The GoI could however consider adding additional criteria to its ECD funding allocation processes, such as the ability to raise revenue at the subnational level, and the number of children in subnational locations. It could also establish more precise formulas for determining funding. These steps could improve fairness in allocations and efficiency by ensuring that funds are allocated where they are most needed. Establishing formula-based allocations also promotes transparency in budgets.

Budget coordination is expected to be strengthened under the HI-ECD policy. Central and local government work plans and budgets are determined according to the National Development Planning System process. Currently, each ministry receives its budget allocation based on the Presidential Regulation and Decree which is issued each fiscal year. The relevant ministries receive allocation for their ECD activities, based on which they set their budgets to implement the ECD tasks and goals in accordance with their respective mandates. When the HI-ECD Policy is fully implemented, ministry budgets and work plans will be more coordinated.

The government is not able to report ECD expenditure in all sectors. The GoI does report ECD spending on education, health, nutrition, and child protection, with figures provided for 2013 in table 2.4. But child and social protection spending for children is not disaggregated by age group; only an overall figure is available for all children up to the age of 18. Adding lines to child and social protection budgets to allow for identification of resources focused on young children would be helpful as the sector grows.

ECD expenditure may not be adequate to provide quality services for all. According to Law No. 20/2003 on the National Education System, a minimum of 20 percent of government spending must be on education. But funding for other sectors, as well as preschool education, may not be sufficient, and funding

Table 2.4   Early Childhood Development Budget across Sectors in Indonesia, 2013

Sector	Budget (IDR)	Budget (USD)	Percentage of GDP
Education	1,569,218,277,000	162,414,000	0.0187
Health	2,743,515,353,000	283,954,000	0.0327
Nutrition	281,488,770,000	29,134,100	0.0034
Child protection	22,206,908,000	2,298,410	0.0003
Social protection	656,087,490,000[a]	67,905,000	0.0078

Source: Budget documents of Education & Health Ministries (2013); the accountability reports of Social Affairs Ministry (2012); and Women Empowerment and Child Protection Ministry (2013).
Note: Currency exchange rate for January 1, 2013, has been used for the conversion of the budget amounts into USD. GDP is for 2013. GDP = gross domestic product; IDR = Indonesian rupiah; USD = US dollar.
a. This figure includes budget from the National Family Planning Coordinating Board (BKKBN) allocated for parenting programs.

for preschools is limited. Box 2.4 summarizes the current status of government spending on ECED services. For example, in 2013, ECCE spending was 0.43 percent out of a total government expenditure on education of Rp 73,087,504,957,000. In 2012, it was 0.56 percent; in 2011, it was 0.79 percent. Evidence from Organisation for Economic Co-operation and Development countries suggest that public investment of at least 1.0 percent of gross domestic product (GDP) is the minimum amount necessary to ensure high-quality early childhood care and education. While higher spending does not guarantee higher quality, the level of investment has implications for access, coverage, and quality. Given the large positive externalities and potential for market failure without government support, public provision is often necessary to reach all children with the services essential to their healthy development.

Out-of-pocket expenditure refers to direct outlays by households, including gratuities and in-kind payments, to service providers. In health, this includes health practitioners and suppliers of pharmaceuticals, therapeutic appliances, and other goods and services whose primary intent is to contribute to the restoration or enhancement of the health status of individuals or population groups. Table 2.5 displays cross-country comparisons of health expenditure. Out-of-pocket health expenditure as a percentage of total health expenditure is at 45 percent according to the World Health Organization (WHO) Global Health Expenditure Database for 2012. This percentage is not too far away from the comparators in the table, but still high for a country with in principle free public health care.

Fees levied for ECD services vary. Some ECCE centers charge numerous types of fees to families, such as tuition, meals, transport, registration, and supplies. Other schools do not charge anything, or do not charge poor families. In the health sector, most services are covered for participants in the national health insurance system (JKN). Those who have not paid JKN insurance premiums, are not yet enrolled, or are not recipients of government health grants to cover premiums must pay for health services, but, as previously mentioned, out-of-pocket costs remain high.

Remuneration for ECD workers varies and may not be adequate. At government institutions, salaries for preprimary teachers entering the field should be

Box 2.4 Current Government Spending on Early Childhood Education and Development

Central government spending on ECED services is low in comparison with other subsectors and unlike these sectors has not grown significantly. In recent years, spending by the central government on ECED has been in the region of Rp 2–3 trillion per year compared to an overall central government budget for education of more than Rp 100 trillion (figure B2.4.1). Perhaps more worrying is that the share of total central government spending on ECED has been declining. In 2011, approximately 4 percent of central government funds were devoted to ECED but by 2013 this share had dropped to around 2 percent.

Figure B2.4.1 Central Government Spending on Early Childhood Education and Development, 2008–13

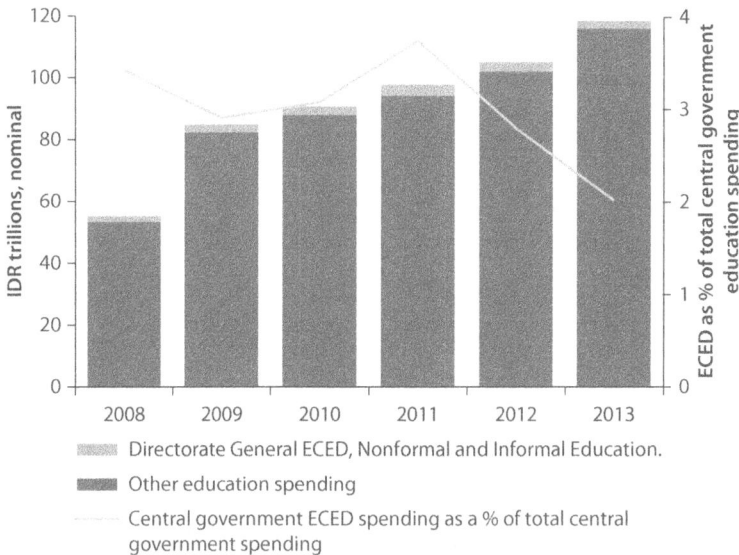

Directorate General ECED, Nonformal and Informal Education.

Other education spending

Central government ECED spending as a % of total central government spending

Note: ECED = early childhood education and development; IDR = Indonesian rupiah.

While local governments contribute substantially to the financing of ECED, the share of total government spending devoted to the subsector remains low because of the focus on financing compulsory basic education and teachers. The last education public expenditure review found that approximately three-quarters of all public spending on ECED came from local governments. However, ECED was still estimated to absorb only around 2 percent of total government (that is central, provincial, and district governments) education spending.

Government spending on ECED remains low in Indonesia compared with other countries—both within the region and around the world. Indonesia spends less than 1 percent of its total education expenditure on preprimary education. In contrast, Vietnam

box continues next page

Box 2.4   Current Government Spending on Early Childhood Education and Development
(continued)

spends 10.8 percent. Low levels of government support to ECED and the size of private sector involvement suggest that the bulk of funding for ECED services in Indonesia come from nongovernment sources.

Source: World Bank 2014.
Note: ECED spending from the Ministry of Religious Affairs is not included. Data on spending from Directorate General ECED taken from Ditjen PAUDNI. Data for total central government spending from audited accounts (2013 is revised budget data).

Table 2.5   Regional Comparison of Selected Health Expenditure Indicators
percent

	Indonesia	China	India	Philippines	Vietnam
Out-of-pocket expenditure as a percentage of all private health expenditure	75	78	86	84	85
Out-of-pocket expenditure as a percentage of total health expenditures	45	34	58	52	49
Government expenditure on health as a percentage of GDP	3	5	4	5	7
Routine Expanded Program Immunization financed by government, 2012	—	—	100	83	34

Source: WHO Global Health Expenditure Database 2012.
Note: GDP = gross domestic product; — = not available.

competitive with salaries for primary teachers entering the field, assuming their education levels are the same. This parity in pay should provide an incentive for talented individuals to enter the ECCE field. Parent and local government contributions pay teachers at community-based preprimary schools, and the average amount varies. Private school teachers are paid a range of salaries depending on the institution. In many countries, preprimary educators are paid less than primary teachers. This discourages individuals from entering the field and contributes to high turnover of staff. Finally, salaries for community-based health workers depend on the location. Some district health offices provide honoraria, in addition to community contributions. It is difficult to gauge if salaries for community-based teachers and health workers are adequate.

On the basis of the aforementioned diagnostic, a number of policy options could be considered to strengthen financing for ECD:

• Use formulas to inform ECD budgets. In addition to the multiple criteria currently considered when determining ECD budgets, consider establishing formulas to set spending levels. This will promote efficiency by ensuring funds go where they are most needed. This also improves transparency by providing clear guidelines on how allocations are made.

- Establish ways to track child and social protection expenditure on ECD. The current system does not disaggregate child and social protection spending on young children from sector spending on all children younger than 18 years of age. Relevant ministries should consider coordinating in developing their ECD budgets. The GoI could put in place a mechanism to allow for identification of ECD-specific spending.
- Increase funding for ECCE. At present the GoI spends a small proportion of the education budget on early childhood education. To ensure that all children attend high-quality preprimary schools, the GoI could consider allocating a higher percentage of its education budget to preprimary education. Recent analyses have shown that the resources required to improve access to better quality ECCE services are within reach but would require increasing ECCE investments among different stakeholders including districts, community development funds, and even by tapping private funds. Box 2.5 indicates some feasible cost projections for a proposed expansion plan for ECED and raising the quality of services provided. In addition, box 2.6 presents potential funding opportunities to improve access to ECED services through the Village Law.

Box 2.5   How Much Would It Cost to Expand Access and Raise the Quality of Early Childhood Education and Development Services for Three- to Six-Year-Olds?

As part of the World Bank's support to Indonesia's medium-term development plan (2015–19), cost estimates were developed to assess the feasibility of proposed expansion plans for ECED. A simple costing model was developed based on three sets of projections. It should be noted that this costing model is not designed to give detailed cost estimates over the plan period but to give a broad indication of the financial feasibility of proposed expansion plans for ECED.

Enrolment projections. The three- to six-year-old age group is used as the basis of enrolment projections. The size of this age group is obtained from overall single-age population projections provided by the UN population division and are based on the 2010 Indonesian population census. Single-age enrolment rates in ECED are taken from Ministry of Education and Culture data. Projections are made by changing the share of children in each age group enrolling in ECED services. The model has been developed for a variety of scenarios for enrolment. The scenario presented here looks at a general expansion of ECED services to ensure that the government's enrollment targets (81 percent of three- to six-year-olds) are met by 2019. Other scenarios considered included the cost of expanding provision only for children in the poorest 40 percent of the population, as well as to children residing in 3T districts. These are not reported here.

Cost projections. Annual teacher costs are based on an average salary for kindergarten teachers (Rp 36 million annually) and playgroup teachers (Rp 12 million annually) based on national teacher registry data (NUPTK) and information from the government's ECED project. Overall, teacher costs for each level are projected using student–educator ratios described in the minimum service standards. An annual cost of Rp 3 million per educator is also included

box continues next page

Box 2.5   How Much Would It Cost to Expand Access and Raise the Quality of Early Childhood Education and Development Services for Three- to Six-Year-Olds? *(continued)*

for professional development activities. Nonteacher costs include a center-based grant (BOP) for each preschool center and ranges from IDR 7 million per playgroup to Rp 11 million per kindergarten. In addition to center-based grants, an amount for the operating costs of centers, resources for purchasing toys and learning materials, as well as the building and up-keep of one playground in each center, are included in the cost estimates. The projections also include the costs of paying salaries of 10 ECED supervisors in each district. Center construction costs are included as one-time expenditure and are based on estimated costs of around Rp 22 million per playgroup and 45 million per kindergarten. The model assumes a maximum center size of 40 children, and the estimates costs are based on existing block grants provided by the Ministry of Education and Culture for these purposes.

Total education cost projections. The final component of the model combines cost and enrolment projections to calculate the overall costs of ECED provision over the next medium-term development plan (2015–19). It assumes that 25 percent of all enrollment occurs in play-groups and 75 percent occurs in kindergartens.

Expanding access to ECED services such that 81 percent of all three- to six-year-olds are enrolled by 2019 would cost on average Rp 50 trillion annually between 2015 and 2019. (See figure B2.5.1) While this is significantly higher than current central and local government support to ECED, it represents approximately 15 percent of government spending on education. This would suggest that the resources required to improve access to better quality ECED services are within reach.

Figure B2.5.1   Estimated Costs of Meeting Enrollment Targets for Three- to Six-Year-Olds with Early Childhood Education and Development Services That Satisfy the Minimum Service Standards

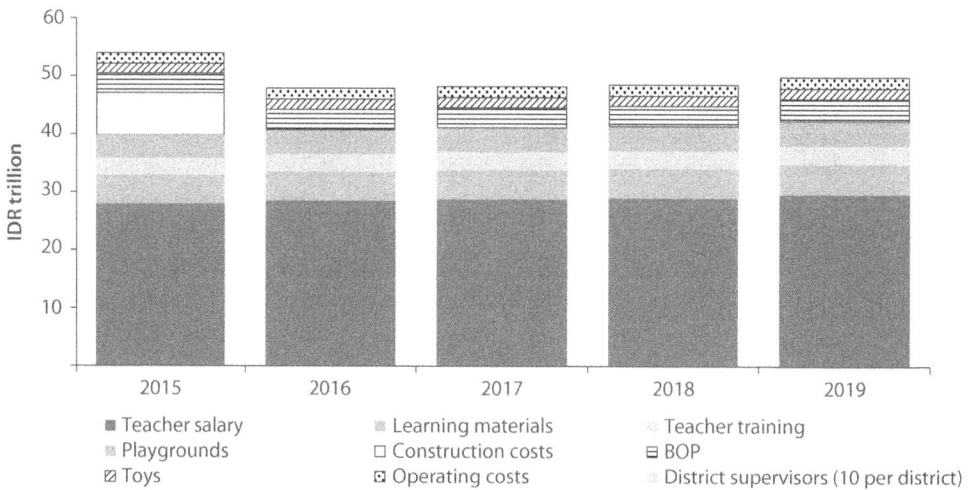

Source: World Bank 2014.

Note: BOP = *Bantuan Operasional PAUD* (government transfer program to support ECED).

Box 2.6 Opportunities to Improve Access to Early Childhood Education and Development Services through the Village Law

In January 2014, the Indonesian Parliament ratified the Law on Village Government (*Undang-Undang Desa*—UU Desa). The UU Desa, or Law 6/2014, envisages a transfer of national and district government resources in an amount estimated at up to US$140,000 per village per year. The law also stipulates that these funds (*dana desa*) should be utilized according to the principles of transparency, accountability, and inclusion—principles operationalized through over 15 years of implementation of the government's community development programs such as Kecamatan Development Program and National Program for Community Empowerment (PNPM Mandiri). The UU Desa represents an enormous opportunity for villages to access resources for local development and poverty reduction efforts. *Dana desa*, if invested effectively, can complement district government investments in basic services, thereby improving access and quality of basic health, education, and infrastructure for rural Indonesians. With strong evidence that attending ECED has great benefit for poor children in preparing them for further education, ECED is a strong candidate for funding by *Dana Desa*.

Source: World Bank 2014.

Policy Goal 2: Implementing Widely

Implementing widely refers to the scope of ECD programs available, the extent of coverage (as a share of the eligible population) and the degree of equity within ECD service provision. By definition, a focus on ECD involves (at a minimum) interventions in health, nutrition, education, and social and child protection and should target pregnant women, young children, and their parents and caregivers. A robust ECD policy should include programs in all essential sectors; provide comparable coverage and equitable access across regions and socioeconomic status—especially reaching the most disadvantaged young children and families.

Policy Lever 2.1: Scope of Programs (Rating: Established)
Effective ECD systems have programs established in all essential sectors and ensure that every child and expecting mother have guaranteed access to the essential services and interventions they need to live healthfully. The scope of programs assesses the extent to which ECD programs across key sectors reach all beneficiaries. Figure 2.3 presents a summary of the key interventions needed to support young children and their families via different sectors at different stages in a child's life.

Figure 2.3   Essential Interventions during Different Periods of Young Children's Development

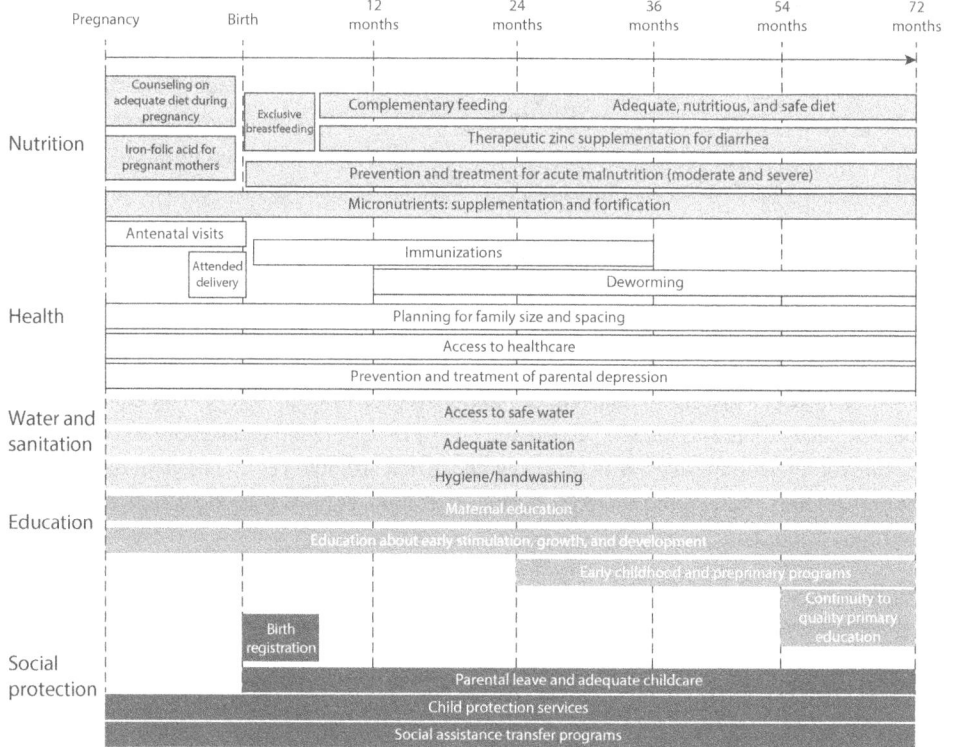

Source: Denboba et al. 2014.
Note: The idea of presenting interventions by sector and/or age has been used by a number of previous authors.

ECD programs are established to target all relevant groups of beneficiaries in Indonesia. As displayed in figure 2.4, Indonesia has a range of ECD programs established in all of the relevant sectors: education, health, nutrition, and social and child protection. Interventions are established that serve pregnant women, young children, and parents and caregivers. In chapter 3, we further discuss the coverage of ECD interventions based on data from the Demographic and Health Surveys (DHS) to present the extent to which ECD programs reach out to families and young children.

The scope of nutrition programs could be expanded. Currently, the Ministry of Health is trying to tackle the prevalence of malnutrition through the Food Infants and Children National Strategy. Besides home visiting programs to provide parents with health information on health and nutrition, the ministry also provides maternal depression screening and services, as well as the referrals. However, the scope of nutrition programs could be expanded to include healthy eating and exercise programs to prevent childhood obesity and feeding programs at centralized locations often available in most communities such as *Posyandus* (integrated village health units). ECD programs are established in all

Figure 2.4 Scope of Early Childhood Development Interventions in Indonesia, by Sector and Target Population

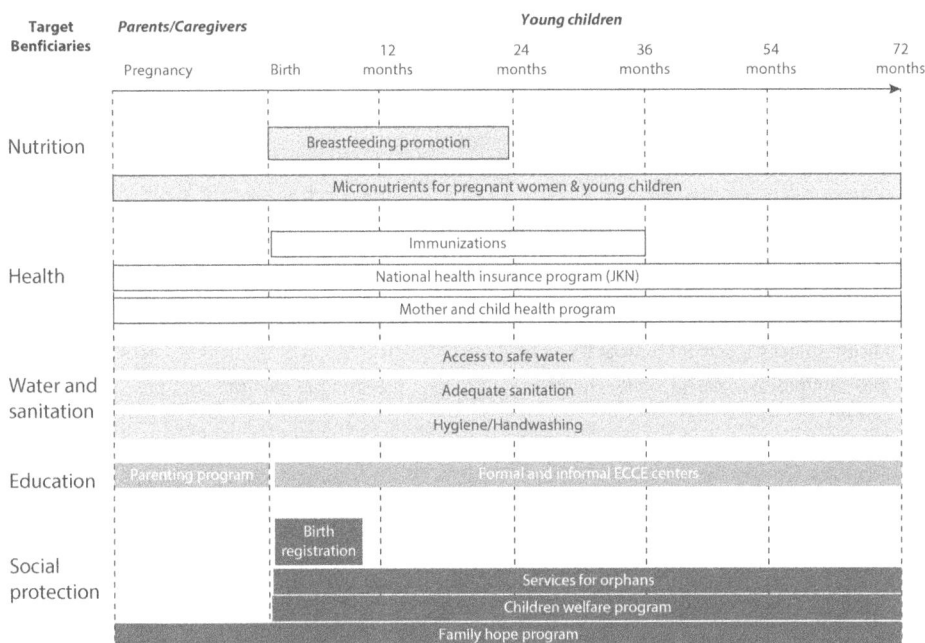

Note: JKN = Jaminan Kesehatan Nasional.

essential areas of focus. A variety of interventions are established in all essential areas of ECD service provision, including in health, nutrition, education, and social and child protection. Key programs are summarized in table 2.6. The table indicates that while a range of ECD interventions exist, coverage is not always universal.

On the basis of the aforementioned diagnostic, a number of policy options could be considered to strengthen the scope of programs for ECD:

• Establish maternal depression screening and treatment to help both mothers and children. Emerging evidence suggests that maternal depression is widespread in low- and middle-income countries. Maternal depression can interfere with bonding and impede responsive caregiving and can have negative lifelong effects on children's cognitive and emotional development. Maternal depression is treatable, often through community-based interventions such as support groups and home visits. Interventions to prevent depression and support mothers can yield high returns.

• Expand the scope of nutrition programs to improve the health of pregnant women and young children while implementing Food, Infants and Children National Strategy widely. The scope of nutrition programs could be expanded to include healthy eating and exercise programs to prevent childhood obesity, food supplements for pregnant women and young children, and feeding

Table 2.6 Early Childhood Development Programs and Coverage in Indonesia

ECD intervention	Coverage
State-sponsored preprimary/kindergarten education	11,256,734 children
State-sponsored early childhood care and education	(3,963,519 in kindergarten; 212,561
Community-based early childhood care and education	in daycare; 3,154,730 in playgroup; 3,925,925 in other type of ECD)
Mosquito bed net distribution for children younger than 7 years of age	—
Antenatal and newborn care	4,631,735 women
Childhood wellness and growth monitoring	16,266,768 children
Comprehensive immunizations	3,929,748 children
Micronutrient support for pregnant women: Ferrous supplementation	4,420,684 women
Micronutrient support for postnatal women	—
Micronutrient support for young children: Vitamin A supplementation	17,675,627 children
Food supplements for young children	—
Food supplements for expecting mothers	—
Breastfeeding promotion programs Breastfeeding and supplementary food counseling	3,929 and 416 women
Feeding programs in preprimary/kindergarten schools	—
Parenting integrated into health/community programs	— (although happens to some degree at HI-ECD services)
Home visiting programs to provide parenting messages	—
Programs for orphans and vulnerable children: Social welfare program for children	172,637 children (1,750 are children with special needs)
Interventions for children with special (emotional and physical) needs	
Antipoverty intervention focused on ECD: Family Hope Program	32,149 pregnant women; 615,460 children younger than five years of age
Integrated services for women and child protection: Integrated services for women and children victims of violence	—

Note: ECD = early childhood development; HI-ECD = Holistic Integrated-Early Childhood Development; — = not available.

programs at preprimary schools. As discussed earlier, stunting among young children is widespread. Providing babies and children with nutritious food or the means to procure it may be one way to reduce stunting.

Policy Lever 2.2: Coverage (Rating: Emerging)

A robust ECD policy should establish programs in all essential sectors, ensure high degrees of coverage and reach the entire population equitably–especially the most disadvantaged young children–so that every child and expecting mother have guaranteed access to essential ECD services. Many but not all pregnant women have access to essential ECD health interventions. The rate of births

Table 2.7   Access to Essential Health Services for Young Children and Pregnant Women
percent

	Indonesia	China	India	Philippines	Vietnam
One-year-old children immunized against DPT (corresponding vaccines: DPT3ß)	64	99	72	86	97
Children younger than five years of age with diarrhea receive oral rehydration/continued feeding (2009–12)	39	—	26	47	47
Children younger than five years of age with suspected pneumonia taken to health care provider (2010)	75	—	69	50	73
Pregnant women receiving antenatal care (at least four times)	88	—	37	78	60

Source: UNICEF Country Statistics 2012.
Note: DPT = diphtheria, pertussis, and tetanus; UNICEF = United Nations Children's Fund; — = not available.

attended by skilled attendants is 83.1 percent, and 88 percent of pregnant women receive at least four prenatal care visits.[2] Until recently, childbirth insurance covered the costs of delivery; deliveries are now covered for participants in the new national health care insurance system. Even without cost as a barrier, there is the possibility that pregnant women may face access issues such as lack of proximity to skilled health professionals. The percentage of pregnant women living with HIV who receive antiretroviral therapy to prevent mother-to-child transmission is not available.

Some young children lack access to basic health interventions. Several access indicators suggest that some young Indonesians do not receive preventive care and appropriate treatment for illnesses. Sixty-four percent of one-year-olds receive a complete course of immunizations against diphtheria, pertussis, and tetanus (DPT) (see table 2.7). Many less developed countries have achieved higher vaccination rates and have established systems to reach marginalized populations in remote areas. Approximately 75 percent of children younger than five years of age with suspected pneumonia are taken to a health care provider, but only 39 percent of children with suspected pneumonia receive antibiotics. Only 3 percent of children in at-risk areas sleep under an insecticide-treated net.

The level of access to nutrition interventions for young children and pregnant women could be expanded. The exclusive breastfeeding rate until the age of six months is 41.5 percent. This suggests that breastfeeding is a fairly widespread practice, but more support for mothers and education on its importance may be necessary. The anemia rate in preschool age children is 28.1 percent, according to the Basic Health Profile, 2013. According to the WHO, that level of prevalence constitutes a moderate public health problem, therefore interventions to expand intake of iron supplement may be necessary. This could be through vitamin supplementation, or iron-fortified products. Efforts to reduce parasitic infections could also lower anemia rates. Since 2008, the law requires that iron be added to flour.

Table 2.8 Access to Essential Nutrition Services for Young Children and Pregnant Women
percent

	Indonesia	China	India	Philippines	Vietnam
Children younger than five years of age with moderate/severe stunting (2008–12)	36	10	48	32	23
Infants exclusively breastfed until 6 months of age	42	28	46	34	17
Infants with low birth weight	9	3	28	21	5
Prevalence of anemia in pregnant women (2005)	44	29	50	44	32
Prevalence of anemia in preschool-age children	45	20	74	36	34

Source: UNICEF Country Statistics, 2012; WHO Global Database on Anemia.

More than 36 percent of children younger than five years of age in Indonesia have moderate to severe stunting (see table 2.8). Stunting is defined as having a height (or length)-for-age more than two standard deviations below the median according to international norms. It is an indicator of chronic malnutrition. Stunting early in life can have long-term effects: it can damage health and reduce an individual's cognitive development, educational performance, and economic productivity. This has negative consequences not only for the well-being of the individual but also for the future success of Indonesia as a country. Given this high figure, interventions to increase the amount and quality of food may be necessary. This could include offering food supplements or programs to make nutritious food more affordable for families. Increasing breastfeeding rates also has the potential to reduce stunting rates, as breastmilk has tremendous nutritional benefits and offers a number of protections against common child health problems. It would likely be an effective and inexpensive approach to reduce stunting rates.

The anemia rate for pregnant women is 37.1 percent, according to the Basic Health Profile, 2013. According to the WHO, that level of prevalence constitutes a moderate public health problem. Anemia can have adverse health effects: mild anemia may impair work productivity, and severe cases can increase risk of maternal and child mortality. Mandated flour fortification, an initiative to provide ferrous supplementation to pregnant women, and better access to medical treatment for parasites have helped reduced the anemia rate in recent years.

Access to early childhood care and education (ECCE) in Indonesia is increasing. The country's gross enrollment rate in preprimary education (five to six years) in 2011 was 46 percent. In 1991, the rate was 16 percent, and in 2002, it was 26 percent. Gross enrollment is defined as the total enrollment in a specific level of education, regardless of age, expressed as a percentage of the official school-age population corresponding to the same level of education in a given school year. It is widely used to show the general level of participation in a given level of education. The average gross enrollment rate for the Asia region for 2011

Table 2.9 Regional Comparison of Level of Access to Birth Registration
percent

	Indonesia	China	India	Philippines	Vietnam
Birth registration	67	—	41	90	95

Source: UNICEF Country Statistics 2005–12.
Note: — = not available.

year was 62 percent. According to the UNESCO Institute for Statistics, ECCE enrollment is higher in China (69.9 percent, 2012), India (58.1 percent, 2011), the Philippines (51.5 percent, 2009), and Vietnam (77.2 percent, 2012) than in Indonesia. The Ministry of Education and Culture has set a target of 75 percent of preschool enrollment in 2015. Scale-up is intended mainly through nonformal and community-based programs.

Birth registration can be a critical first step to reach children with the services they need and protect them against exploitation. While the GoI mandates birth registration, only 67 percent of Indonesian newborns are registered at birth compared with 90 percent in the Philippines and 95 percent in Vietnam (77.2 percent, 2012) as shown in table 2.9. Building on the free birth certification service established by the government, improved efforts are needed to universalize birth registration and accelerate the issuance of birth certificates.

On the basis of this diagnostic, a number of policy options could be considered to strengthen the coverage of programs for ECD:

- Examine why access to medical care for pregnant women is not higher despite free services. According to UNICEF data, nearly one in five women in Indonesia gives birth without a skilled attendant present. Until recently, childbirth insurance covered the cost of the services and now the JKN covers it. Examine why despite free provision some women do not receive this essential medical care. It may be lack of access to skilled practitioners, lack of education on the importance of appropriate medical care, or other reasons.
- Consider covering all pregnant women in the new scheme insurance. The transition of maternity health insurance (*Jaminan Persalinan, Jampersal*) schemes into national health insurance (*Jaminan Kesehatan Nasional*, JKN) has resulted in lower access among pregnant women to birth insurance. During the *Jampersal* era, all pregnant women regardless of their socioeconomic status were eligible for free birthing insurance. Because of cost burden, the uncovered pregnant women, especially in disadvantaged areas, tend to go back to traditional birth attendants. Universal birthing insurance will lower the rate of maternal and infant mortality.
- Expand nutrition programs to address widespread stunting and nutrient deficits among children. More than one-third of Indonesian children younger than five years of age are stunted. This indicates that chronic malnutrition is a fact of life for many of the country's youngest citizens. A multifaceted approach may be necessary to address this issue. Food and micronutrients

supplements, income supports, increased breastfeeding rates, and nutrition education may be necessary.

• Continue to increase ECCE enrollment, while also establishing or maintaining quality. While it has increased in recent years, preschool attendance in Indonesia is still lagging. Continue efforts to expand enrollment through a variety of formal and nonformal programs.

Policy Lever 2.3: Equity (Rating: Emerging)

On the basis of the robust evidence of the positive effects ECD interventions can have for children from disadvantaged backgrounds, every government should pay special attention to equitable provision of ECD services (for example, Engle et al 2011; Naudeau et al. 2011). One of the fundamental goals of any ECD policy should be to provide equitable opportunities to all young children and their families.

Boys and girls attend preprimary school at nearly the same rate. But attendance by poor children is far lower than the national average. In 2011, the gross enrollment rate for preprimary school was 45 percent for boys and 46 percent for girls. In the poorest quintile, there are 8,077,590 children age five years and younger. Of those, 1,029,489 are enrolled in an ECCE center of any kind. The ECCE enrollment rate for the poorest fifth of the population is approximately 12.7 percent. This is far below the national enrollment average of 46 percent. School fees, lack of accessible schools in poorer areas, low quality, and lack of knowledge about the importance of preschool may be barriers to attendance for children from poor families. Of the children from poor families who do attend preschool, it is difficult to gauge if the quality of the schools they attend is equal to the quality of schools attended by wealthier children.

Children with special needs may not have full access to preschool. Under the national education law every child is entitled to a quality education for nine years, and the government must provide inclusive education and special services for children with special needs. Preprimary attendance is not required or free in Indonesia, and guarantees of access do not exist for preschool aged children with special needs. Government data state that there are 112,000 children with special needs in Indonesia, but it is not known how many attend preprimary school (Ministry of Women Empowerment and Child Protection and Central Bureau of Statistics 2012). The HI-ECD policy has the goal of providing quality ECD services, including education, to all children, including children with special needs. Currently, there are few mechanisms in place to implement this policy goal. Accessible facilities, staff training, and identification of children with special needs will all be necessary to provide all children with appropriate services.

Access to ECD services varies by economic status and geographical location. The birth registration ratio between the richest 20 percent of the Indonesian population and the poorest 20 percent is 2.2 (see figure 2.5). While 97 percent of women from the highest income quintile have a skilled attendant at delivery, only 58 percent of women from the poorest quintile do.

Figure 2.5 Disparities between Bottom and Top Quintiles of Wealth

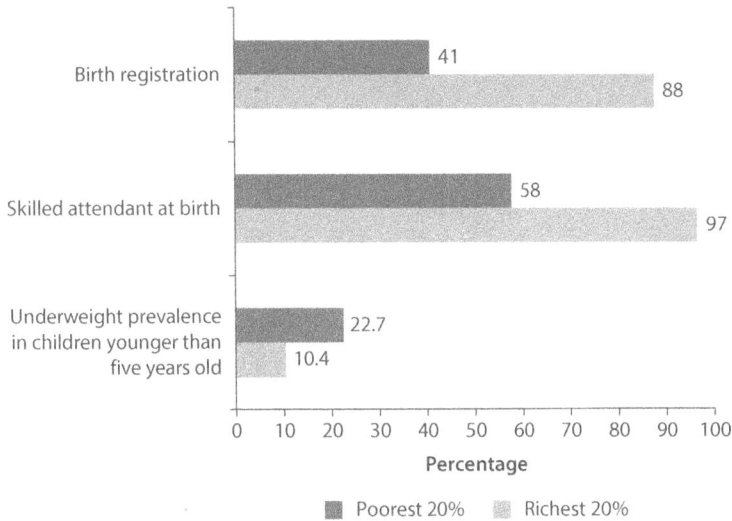

Birth registration: 41 (Poorest 20%), 88 (Richest 20%)
Skilled attendant at birth: 58 (Poorest 20%), 97 (Richest 20%)
Underweight prevalence in children younger than five years old: 22.7 (Poorest 20%), 10.4 (Richest 20%)

Percentage

■ Poorest 20% ▨ Richest 20%

Source: UNICEF Multiple Indicator Cluster Survey 2008–12.

Figure 2.6 Disparities between Urban and Rural Areas

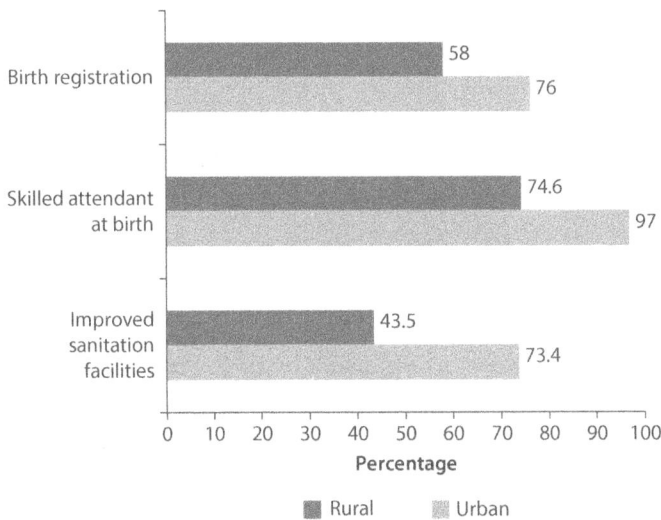

Birth registration: 58 (Rural), 76 (Urban)
Skilled attendant at birth: 74.6 (Rural), 97 (Urban)
Improved sanitation facilities: 43.5 (Rural), 73.4 (Urban)

Percentage

■ Rural ▨ Urban

Source: UNICEF Multiple Indicator Cluster Survey 2008–12.

While having appropriate medical personnel at childbirth is nearly universal for wealthy women, just less than half of poor women have no one skilled to care for them and their babies at childbirth. Children younger than five years of age who are underweight are 2.2 times more common among families in the poorest quintile than among the wealthiest quintile.

Disparities in access to ECD services exist between urban and rural areas, although they are not as vast as those by household wealth. Birth registration is higher in urban areas than in rural areas (see figure 2.6). Skilled personnel attend deliveries in urban areas at the rate of 91.8 percent and 74.6 percent in rural areas. The underweight prevalence in children younger than five years of age is 15.2 percent among children in urban areas versus 20.7 percent among children in rural areas. In urban areas, 73.4 percent of residents use improved sanitation facilities; the rate is 43.5 percent in rural areas.

On the basis of the aforementioned diagnostic, a number of policy options could be considered to strengthen equity in programs for ECD:

- Address the large inequities in access to ECD services between rich and poor families and families in urban and remote areas. Children from poor families face numerous disadvantages starting even before birth. These inequalities early in life widen over time if effective interventions are not implemented. Addressing inequality early in life is effective and cost efficient. Investments in ECD are crucial to ensure that all children have the opportunity to develop their full potential. Increasing coverage rates for services may address some of these disparities. Improving quality of services may also reduce inequities, as the quality of services received by poor families may be lower than those received by wealthier families.
- Examine whether mechanisms exist to provide quality ECD services for children with special needs. While children with special needs are guaranteed access to education and other ECD services under the law, it is not clear that appropriate programs exist to serve all children who need them. Training personnel, upgrading facilities, and establishing ways to identify children in need of special services may be necessary.

Policy Goal 3: Monitoring and Assuring Quality

Monitoring and assuring quality refers to the existence of information systems to monitor access to ECD services and outcomes across children, standards for ECD services and systems to monitor and enforce compliance with those standards. Ensuring the quality of ECD interventions is vital because evidence has shown that unless programs are of high quality, the impact on children can be negligible, or even detrimental.

Policy Lever 3.1: Data Availability (Rating: Established)

Accurate, comprehensive, and timely data collection can promote more effective policy making. Well-developed information systems can improve decision making. In particular, data can inform policy choices regarding the volume and allocation of public financing, staff recruitment and training, program quality, adherence to standards, and efforts to target children most in need.

Early Childhood Education and Development in Indonesia • http://dx.doi.org/10.1596/978-1-4648-0646-9

The GoI collects a wide range of administrative data on access to ECD. Administrative data reflect total uptake of services and are gathered through either a census or records made upon receipt of service. Across all sectors, the government collects data on enrollment and training of service providers. Health centers issue monthly reports, with information on usage of health services and nutrition interventions by children by children's age. Health centers do not collect data on usage by socioeconomic status, ethnic background, or children's residence in an urban or rural location. The Ministry of Social Affairs and Ministry of Woman Empowerment and Child Protection have data on the number of cases in the children protection system. However, the data are differently collected between ministries and sometimes outdated.

In the ECCE sector, limited data are collected to track background characteristics and child outcomes. Data on education enrollment by urban/rural location, province, gender, and socioeconomic background are tracked. The GoI does not collect education enrollment data by ethnic background, mother tongue, or special needs status. The GoI has data on the number of ECD-aged children with special needs, but does not collect information on how many of those children are enrolled in ECCE centers.

The GoI collects many types of survey data on ECD access and outcomes. Indonesia participates in UNICEF's Multiple Indicator Cluster Survey (MICS). The survey yields estimates on a number of indicators of children's well-being in a country, including those related to education, health, and child protection. The survey findings allow for comparison of access and outcomes by household wealth and urban/rural location. Recently, the MICS added a new subset of indicators on early childhood development. These data will provide a measure of children's developmental status across multiple domains. Indonesia could collect survey data on these indicators to provide a more nuanced picture of the country's young children.

Individual children's development outcomes are not tracked. The GoI does not track children's individual development outcomes in any systematic way. It does not track children's outcomes in preprimary education. While strong in other types of data collection, Indonesia could benefit from establishing a system to collect and analyze information on individual children's developmental outcomes across several domains: physical, cognitive, socioemotional, and linguistic. Development should be assessed as comprehensively as possible whenever feasible because a child's development in one domain often acts as a catalyst for development in another. The information can be used to establish a baseline and document the magnitude of a problem, identify children requiring referrals for additional services, assess the specific types of ECD interventions that are most and cost effective in a given context or for specific populations, and inform policy dialogue for future planning.

On the basis of the aforementioned diagnostic, a number of policy options could be considered to strengthen data availability for ECD:

- Monitor individual child development outcomes. Given the holistic nature of children's development, it is important to monitor their development as comprehensively as possible. Gathering and monitoring information in one accessible file can help identify children in need interventions. A comprehensive monitoring system will also help evaluate progress under the HI-ECD policy and identify issues that need more efforts.
- Monitoring individual outcomes at health sector is at advanced level through early detection program (*Stimulasi dan Intervensi Dini Tumbuh Kembang*, SDIDTK) held by the Ministry of Health. However, the implementation should be routinely done across Indonesia by providing the qualified health workers.
- Participate in gathering MICS ECD subindicators. MICS data yield a rich snapshot of the state of a country's children. The new subset of MICS ECD subindicators should provide information useful to policy makers.

Policy Lever 3.2: Quality Standards (Rating: Established)

Ensuring quality ECD service provision is essential. A focus on access—without a commensurate focus on ensuring quality—jeopardizes the very benefits that

Table 2.10 Availability of Data to Monitor Early Childhood Development in Indonesia

Administrative data	
Indicator	Tracked
ECCE enrollment rates by region	✓
Number of special needs children enrolled in ECCE	✗
Number of children attending well-child visits	✓
Number of children benefitting from public nutrition interventions	✓
Number of women receiving prenatal nutrition interventions	✓
Number of children enrolled in ECCE by subnational region	✓
Average per student-to-teacher ratio in public ECCE	✓
Is ECCE spending in education sector differentiated within education budget?	✓
Is ECD spending in health sector differentiated within health budget?	✓

Survey data	
Indicator (%)	Tracked
Population consuming iodized salt	✓
Vitamin A supplementation rate for children 6–59 months	✓
Anemia prevalence amongst pregnant women	✓
Children younger than five years of age registered at birth	✓
Children immunized against DPT3 at age 12 months	✓
Pregnant women who attend four antenatal visits	✓
Children enrolled in ECCE by socioeconomic status	✗

Note: ECD = early childhood development; ECCE = early childhood care and education; DPT = diphtheria, pertussis, and tetanus.

policy makers hope children will gain through ECD interventions. The quality of ECD programs is directly related to better cognitive and social development in children (for example, Bryce et al. 2003; Naudeau et al. 2011; Victoria et al. 2008).

Learning standards are established for ECCE. A new curriculum is under development. The Regulation of the Education and Culture Minister No. 58/2009 lays out what young children should learn and know according to their age. The standards, which were established by the Board of National Standards of Education, cover cognitive development, language skills, socioemotional development, physical development, motor skills, arts, religion, and morality.

The Ministry of Education and Culture is developing a new curriculum, which it will endorse when it is ready for implementation. The Regulation of the Education and Culture Minister No. 58/2009, the Generic Menu for ECE Learning, and the Guidelines for Providing ECED Services inform the current curriculum. The kindergarten and Grade 1 curricula are coherent and continuous, with roughly similar core competencies and themes.

Professional qualification requirements for ECCE educators and caregivers exist. The Regulation of Education and Culture Minister No. 16/2007 on Teachers' Academic Qualification and Competencies requires that teachers in formal ECCE centers hold at minimum a postsecondary degree in ECD or psychology. The degree can be either a D-4 (four-year diploma) or an S-1 (bachelor's degree). The Regulation of the Education and Culture Minister No. 58/2009 on Early Child Education Standards requires that teacher assistants, who work primarily in nonformal ECCE centers, must have some postsecondary training specialized in ECD. This can be either at D-2 (two-year diploma) from an accredited training institution, or graduation from secondary school plus an ECD certificate from an accredited training institution. The same regulation requires that caregivers (mostly in nonformal centers) have graduated from secondary school or another similar level of education.

Educators have some opportunities for professional development. Block grants fund ECD teacher associations and private education institutions to conduct teacher training programs. One type of course offers an upgrade to educators' academic qualification. The Directorate of Teachers and Education Personnel manages a basic-level 48-hour course, an intermediate-level 64-hour course, and an advanced 80-hour course. These courses cover health, nutrition, cognitive development, social and emotional development, inclusive education, parenting, curriculum, and learning plans. In-service training is not mandatory. However, because of capacity constraints, these training programs are not available to all educators who may want to participate. Candidates for teaching degrees must complete a preservice practicum.

Infrastructure and service delivery standards are established for ECCE centers. The Minister of Education and Culture Regulation No. 58/2009 on Early Child Education Standards sets child-to-teacher ratio requirements for ECCE centers.

The child-to-teacher ratio standards are as follows: 15:1 for five-year-old children; 12:1 for four-year-old children; 10:1 for three-year-old children; 8:1 for two-year-old children; 6:1 for one-year-old children; and 4:1 for children younger than 12 months. These figures are roughly in line with those in many Organisation for Economic Co-operation and Development countries.

ECCE centers must be open for a minimum number of hours according to Indonesian standards. For children younger than 24 months old, centers should provide 120 minutes of education per week. Children between 24 and 48 months should be able to attend 180 minutes per day, two days a week. Children between 48 and 72 months attending formal ECCE centers should have 150 to 180 minutes per day of school for five or six days per week. At informal centers, children of the same age should be able to attend 180 minutes per day, three days a week.

Under the Regulation of Education and Culture Minister No. 58/2009 on Early Childhood Education Standards, ECCE centers must have at least 3 meters square of interior space per child. Centers must also have hygienic toilet facilities. Daycare centers must have areas for sleeping, eating, and bathing. Educational toys should be available, as well as appropriate indoor and outdoor play spaces. To obtain an ECCE operational permit, centers must provide toilets, a water supply, sanitation systems, and washbasins.

The Ministry of Public Works, Directorate General of Building issues construction standards and permits applicable to all buildings in the country. There are no construction standards specific to ECCE centers. The standards cover necessary aspects of safe and appropriate facilities, except for access to potable water. Permits for new construction require submission of detailed construction plans. Health facilities must also comply with construction standards.

There are established registration and accreditation procedures for ECCE facilities. Both formal and nonformal ECCE centers are required to be accredited. The Minister of Education and Culture Regulation No. 52/2009 on kindergarten accreditation establishes procedures forkindergartens, and the National Accreditation Board for Non-formal Education has an accreditation instrument for nonformal centers. Accreditation renewal occurs every three years, at which point announced inspections are conducted.

On the basis of the aforementioned diagnostic, a number of policy options could be considered to strengthen quality standards for ECD:

- Expand in-service training and professional development opportunities for ECCE educators. Currently, in-service training programs are not widely available, nor is any kind of professional development mandatory. Consider mandating participation in accessible, relevant training.
- Increase the minimum hours at ECCE hours to improve quality. Program intensity matters for quality. International best practice suggests a program of at least 15 hours per week for three-year-olds. While ECCE enrollment is expanding, if the program intensity is too low, the impact may be limited.

- Establish ECED training for health workers (for example, *Posyandu* cadres and village midwives) by combining health, parenting, and early stimulation materials. This has contributed to the quality of integrated ECD services.

Policy Lever 3.3: Compliance with Standards (Rating: Latent)

Establishing standards is essential to providing quality ECD services and to promoting the healthy development of children. Once standards have been established, it is critical that mechanisms are put in place to ensure compliance with standards.

Some ECCE teachers comply with qualifications standards and training requirements. There are 433,081 ECCE educators according to government data (Buku Data PAUDNI 2012). Almost 15 percent have a bachelor's degree or higher. Approximately 25 percent have postsecondary schooling, but not a full four-year degree, and for approximately 39 percent of educators, the highest level of educational attainment is upper secondary school. About 3 percent have completed only lower secondary school. Qualification requirements differ according to the age of children in a classroom, and those figures do not indicate with which age group these educators work, so it is somewhat difficult to gauge compliance with qualifications standards. Nevertheless, these figures do indicate that compliance is far from universal. Roughly 5 percent of these educators participated in in-service training in recent years.

Some ECCE facilities comply with service delivery and infrastructure standards. The average child-to-teacher ratio across ECCE centers in Indonesia is 8:1. Ratios for different age groups are not available, so it is difficult to assess fully if ratios comply with standards. However, it is likely that most centers comply, and some may even have lower ratios. The average number of hours ECCE facilities are open per week is between one and three hours. Again, because that average does not differentiate between age groups served, it is difficult to gauge compliance with the standard, but it seems likely that many centers do not adhere to the minimum opening hours.

The ECE Directorate and district Public Works Offices do not collect data on how many ECCE facilities have construction permits and comply with infrastructure standards. It is likely that formal education centers comply with infrastructure requirements, but the level of compliance in nonformal centers is less clear. Data are not disaggregated by state and nonstate facilities.

Most ECCE facilities are not accredited. In 2012, there were 10,077 accredited ECCE centers in Indonesia, and 152,671 nonaccredited centers. This means that only 6 percent of facilities are accredited. Quality may be lower at nonaccredited schools. More urgently, children's safety may be at risk. Unsafe facilities and lack of staff to supervise and care for children can endanger children.

On the basis of the aforementioned diagnostic, a number of policy options could be considered to strengthen compliance with standards for ECD:

- Ensure that ECCE educators are qualified, particularly at nonformal centers. Consider why many ECCE staff do not meet the qualifications requirements. It may be that educational opportunities are too expensive or not accessible to them, or there may be few incentives to qualification for both individuals and the centers that employ them.
- Examine why ECCE center accreditation rates are so low. The failure of most childcare centers to meet standards for accreditation is cause for concern about both program quality and children's safety. The GoI could examine the reasons behind this. It may be that there are no enforcement mechanisms for failure to comply, costs and procedures to apply and comply are prohibitive, and/or there are inadequate inspectors and personnel to guide centers to meet requirements.
- Revitalize the role of the supervisor in quality assurance. ECED supervisor (*Penilik*) is the one who, by Minister of State Apparatus and Bureaucracy Reform No. 14/2010, is responsible for delivering quality assurance for ECED services. This can be done through capacity building for the supervisor, the development of tools, such as monitoring and evaluation tool to support them in the delivery of their role in quality assurance, and better institutional and organizational supports for supervisor.
- Establish an accreditation system with rating. It is urgently important for the achievement of quality ECED services. With the provision of rating, stage of quality services could be determined.

Benchmarking

Overall, table 2.11 presents the classification of ECD policy in Indonesia within each of the nine policy levers and three policy goals. The SABER-ECD classification system does not rank countries according to any overall scoring; rather, it is intended to share information on how different ECD systems address the same policy challenges. Table 2.12 presents the status of ECD

Table 2.11   Benchmarking Early Childhood Development Policy in Indonesia

Policy goal	Level of development	Policy lever	Level of development
Establishing an enabling environment	●●●○	Legal framework	●●●○
		Intersectoral coordination	●●●○
		Finance	●●●○
Implementing widely	●●○○	Scope of programs	●●●○
		Coverage	●●○○
		Equity	●●○○
Monitoring and assuring quality	●●○○	Data availability	●●●○
		Quality standards	●●●○
		Compliance with standards	●○○○

●○○○ **Latent**   ●●○○ **Emerging**   ●●●○ **Established**   ●●●● **Advanced**

policy development in Indonesia alongside a selection of other countries (a more detailed comparison is provided in chapter 3). Sweden is home to one of the world's most comprehensive and developed ECD policies and achieves a benchmarking of "Advanced" in all nine policy levers. Indonesia is on average on par (slightly higher or lower in terms of average rating) with countries such as Chile and Turkey. On the Compliance with Standards policy lever, it ranks lower than these four countries.

It is important however to note that the existence of laws and policies alone do not always guarantee a correlation with desired ECD outcomes. In many countries, policies on paper and the reality of access and service delivery on the ground are not aligned.

Table 2.13 compares ECD policies in Indonesia with ECD outcomes. The GoI has mandated many key policies, but policy implementation has not always been highly successful. Despite requirements for childhood immunizations and birth registration, roughly one-third of child are not fully immunized or registered at

Table 2.12 Comparison of Indonesia Ratings with Selected Other Countries

		Level of development				
Policy goal	Policy lever	Indonesia	Australia	Chile	Sweden	Turkey
Establishing an enabling environment	Legal framework	●●●○	●●●●	●●●○	●●●●	●●●○
	Coordination	●●●○	●●●●	●●●○	●●●●	●●○○
	Finance	●●●○	●●●●	●●●○	●●●●	●●○○
Implementing widely	Scope of programs	●●●○	●●●○	●●●●	●●●●	●●●○
	Coverage	●●○○	●●●●	●●●○	●●●●	●●○○
	Equity	●●○○	●●●○	●●○○	●●●●	●●○○
Monitoring and assuring quality	Data availability	●●●○	●●●○	●●●○	●●●●	●●○○
	Quality standards	●●●○	●●●○	●●○○	●●●●	●●●○
	Compliance with standards	●○○○	●●●○	●●○○	●●●●	●●○○

●○○○ Latent	●●○○ Emerging	●●●○ Established	●●●● Advanced

Table 2.13 Comparing Early Childhood Development Policies with Outcomes in Indonesia

Policy	Outcomes
Law complies with the International Code of Marketing of Breast Milk Substitutes	Exclusive breastfeeding rate (>6 months): 41.5%
Indonesia has national policy to encourage the iodization of salt	Household iodized salt consumption 62.3%
Preprimary school is not compulsory and often not free	Preprimary school enrollment: 46%
Young children are required to receive a complete course of childhood immunizations	Children with DPT (12–23 months): 64%
Policy mandates the registration of children at birth in Indonesia	Completeness of birth registration: 67%

Note: DPT = diphtheria, pertussis, and tetanus.

Early Childhood Education and Development in Indonesia · http://dx.doi.org/10.1596/978-1-4648-0646-9

birth. Notably, even without mandatory preprimary attendance and fees at many programs, almost half of children attend some kind of ECCE program. This is encouraging, and suggests that with expanded access children will continue to attend preschool at higher rates.

Conclusion

The SABER-ECD initiative was designed to enable ECD policy makers and development partners to identify opportunities for further development of effective ECD systems. This chapter has presented a framework to compare Indonesia's ECD system with other countries in the region and internationally. Each of the nine policy levers was examined in detail, and some policy options were identified to strengthen ECD. The main conclusions are as follows:

- Establishing an enabling environment: Indonesia has enacted many key laws to ensure young children's well-being. The HI-ECD policy is an important step to expand access to and quality of essential ECD services. Funding for the sector may be inadequate.
- Implementing widely: The scope of ECD programs in Indonesia is generally broad, but could be expanded, particularly in nutrition. Coverage rates to some services need improvement. Childhood malnutrition rates are high in the country. Vast disparities in services and outcomes exist between wealthier and poorer families, as well as between families living in urban and rural locations. Children with special needs may not have access to appropriate services, despite policy goals to provide inclusive service.
- Monitoring and assuring quality: Indonesia collects a wide variety of administrative and survey data. The government has established many important ECD delivery and infrastructure standards. Some teachers do not comply with qualifications requirements, and only a small percentage of ECCE centers are accredited.

Table 2.14 summarizes the key policy options identified to inform policy dialogue and improve the provision of essential ECD services in Indonesia. The HI-ECD policy shows a commitment to improving services for young children in the country. The challenge to address disparities between rich and poor, low access to services, and quality issues will be largely in implementation. The policy options are classified into short- and medium-term options according to potentially required implementation timeframe.

Table 2.14 Summary of Policy Options to Improve Early Childhood Development Policy Development in Indonesia

Short term (within 2 years)	Medium term (3–5 years)
1. Establishing an enabling environment	
Use formulas (such as capitation, but possibly with targeting to the most vulnerable as well) to inform ECD budgets to improve efficiency and transparency.	Socialize the issuance of HI-ECD policy to local level, along with technical guidance for its implementation.
Establish mechanisms for coordination at the national level between state and nonstate stakeholders, as well as cost-sharing for multisectoral agencies that are part of the HI-ECD program.	Mandate attendance in quality preprimary education for children ages 3–6 years.
Strengthen communication across sectors through the co-ordination meetings held by HI-ECD national task force.	Extend maternity and paternity leave to allow parents greater flexibility for labor-force participation and proper caregiving for infants, also make maternity period more flexible.
Establish ways to track child and social protection expenditures for ECD-aged children.	Increase funding for early childhood care and education to ensure quality and access.
Make mandatory the immunization course for mumps, rubella, and meningitis.	
2. Implementing widely	
Examine whether mechanisms exist to provide quality ECD services for children with special needs.	Establish maternal depression screening and treatment to help both mothers and children.
Give communities incentives to experiment with approaches to providing integrated ECD services using existing infrastructure.	Expand nutrition programs to address stunting and nutrient deficits among children
	Consider covering all pregnant women in the new insurance scheme (*Jaminan Kesehatan Nasional, JKN*).
	Continue to increase preprimary enrollment, while also addressing quality issues.
	Address the large inequities in access to ECD services between rich and poor families, and families in urban and remote areas.
3. Monitoring and assuring quality	
Examine why ECED center accreditation rates are so low.	Monitor individual child development outcomes.
Establish an accreditation system with quality ratings.	Establish an advanced system to monitor individual health outcomes through early detection program (*Stimulasi dan Intervensi Dini Tumbuh Kembang*, SDIDTK).
Revitalize the role of ECD supervisors in quality assurance.	Expand in-service training and professional development opportunities for early childhood educators
Broaden training for health workers (for example, *Posyandu* cadre and village midwives) by combining attention to health, parenting, and early stimulation.	Ensure that early childhood educators are qualified, particularly in nonformal centers.
	Increase the minimum hours of attendance at centers to increase dosage and improve quality.

Note: ECD = early childhood development; HI-ECD = Holistic Integrated-Early Childhood Development.

Notes

1. Indonesian National AIDS Commission, 2012. Republic of Indonesia Country Report on the Follow up to the Declaration of Commitment on HIV/AIDS (UNGASS). Reporting Period 2010. http://www.unaids.org/en/dataanalysis/knowyourresponse/countryprogressreports/2012countries/ce_ID_Narrative_Report.pdf.

2. These figures are from UNICEF's Multiple Indicator Cluster Survey 2008–2012 (used throughout this report for cross-country comparability reason). Yet, the Indonesia Health Profile 2012 states that 88.6 percent of births are delivered in the presence of skilled attendants and 90.1 percent of pregnant women receive at least four prenatal care visits.

CHAPTER 3

Coverage of Interventions at the Provincial Level

Janice Heejin Kim and Quentin Wodon

Abstract

In the Systems Approach for Better Education Results-Early Childhood Development (SABER-ECD) framework, the second policy goal refers to the extent to which policies and programs are implemented widely. Questions are asked as to the scope of the programs being implemented, their coverage, and the equity in coverage between groups or regions. This chapter digs deeper into the question of whether essential ECD interventions are implemented in the country, with a focus on differences between provinces in coverage rates. On the basis of a framework identifying 25 essential interventions for young children, the chapter provides data on national and provincial level coverage. The 25 interventions are grouped into five packages defined in terms of when the interventions should be implemented: the pregnancy, birth, child health, preschool, and family support packages. Overall, information is available in the household surveys for 19 of the 25 interventions considered, so the diagnostic provided is fairly comprehensive.

Introduction

The objective of this chapter, which provides summary results from a more detailed study (Heejin Kim and Wodon 2015), is to document the extent to which children and families benefit from essential early childhood development (ECD) interventions in Indonesia, focusing on differences in coverage between provinces. The framework follows Denboba et al. (2014), who identify 25 essential ECD interventions, most of which can be tracked using secondary data originated from household surveys, and especially Demographic and Health Surveys. This framework is not unique, and other efforts have been made to think through investments in ECD (see, for example, Britto et al. 2013, as well as Naudeau et al. (2011), about entry points for effective ECD programs). But the framework suggested by Denboba et al. has the benefit of being simple and useful for organizing descriptive empirical work on the coverage of various interventions.

The chapter is structured as follows: chapter 2 introduces the 25 ECD interventions and documents the sources of data used for the coverage analysis. This chapter presents the data on the coverage of essential interventions. Chapter 4 discusses the relationship between coverage levels and the level of economic development of the provinces. A brief conclusion follows.

Framework and Data

The 25 essential interventions proposed by Denboba et al. (2014) is provided in figure 3.1, both according to the sectors to which the interventions belong and the time period in the life of children to which they apply. In terms of time periods, the interventions can be grouped into five packages: the pregnancy, birth, child health, preschool, and family support packages. As noted in box 3.1, these interventions have been shown to have high returns.

The assessment of the coverage of the 25 interventions is based for most interventions on publicly available data from the 2002, 2007, and 2012 Demographic and Health Surveys. In the case of interventions for the preschool package, the information is based on data from the 2007 and 2012 SUSENAS surveys. All these surveys are representative at the provincial level, hence this is the level at

Figure 3.1 Essential Interventions for Young Children

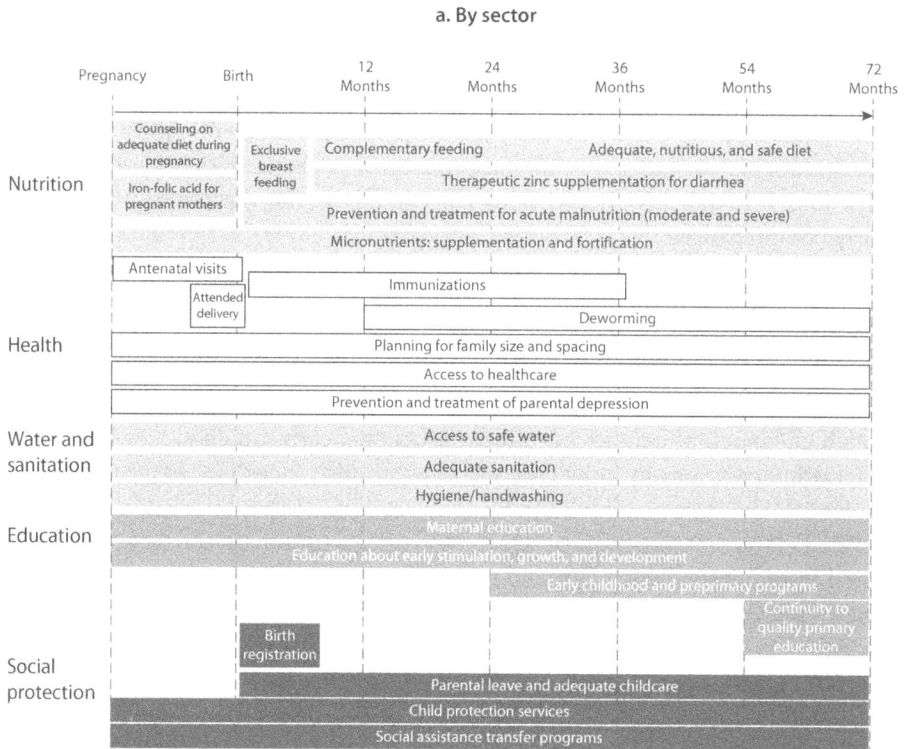

a. By sector

Source: Denboba et al. 2014.

Figure 3.1 Essential Interventions for Young Children *(continued)*

b. By age

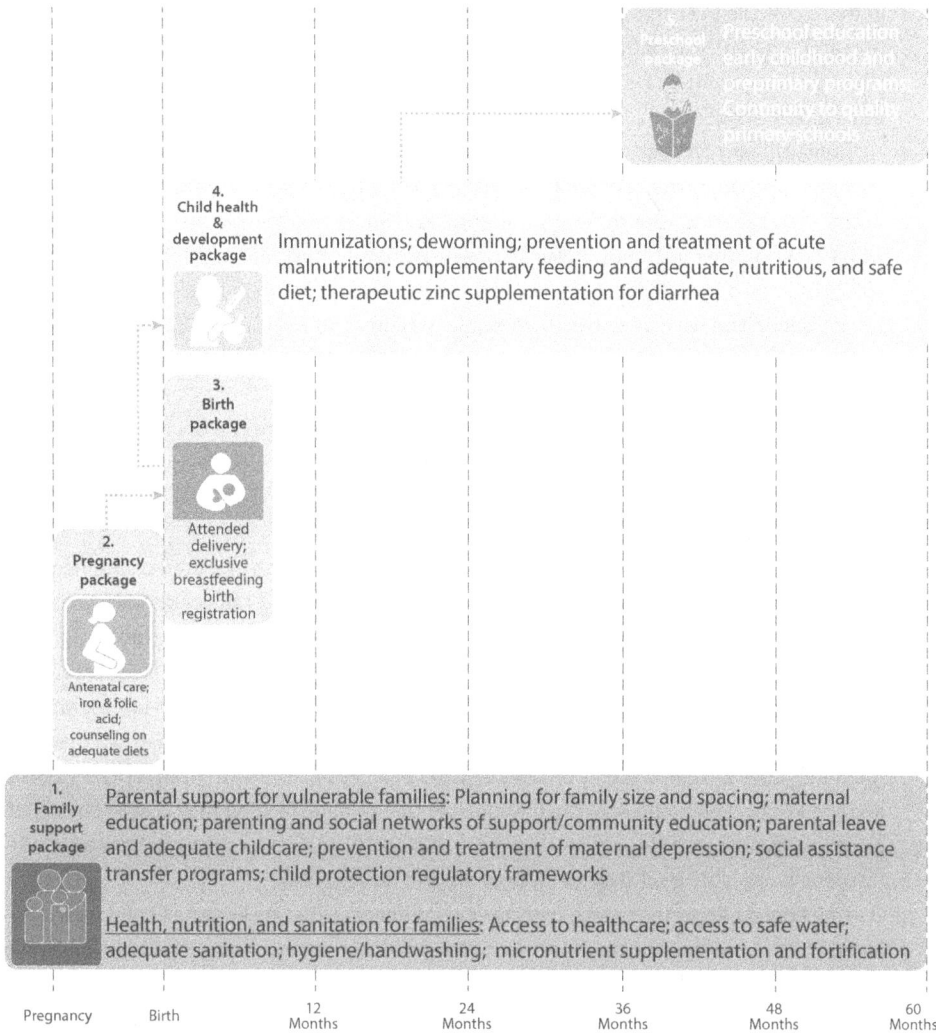

5. Preschool package Preschool education; early childhood and prepimary programs; Continuity to quality primary schools

4. Child health & development package Immunizations; deworming; prevention and treatment of acute malnutrition; complementary feeding and adequate, nutritious, and safe diet; therapeutic zinc supplementation for diarrhea

3. Birth package Attended delivery; exclusive breastfeeding birth registration

2. Pregnancy package Antenatal care; iron & folic acid; counseling on adequate diets

1. Family support package

Parental support for vulnerable families: Planning for family size and spacing; maternal education; parenting and social networks of support/community education; parental leave and adequate childcare; prevention and treatment of maternal depression; social assistance transfer programs; child protection regulatory frameworks

Health, nutrition, and sanitation for families: Access to healthcare; access to safe water; adequate sanitation; hygiene/handwashing; micronutrient supplementation and fortification

Pregnancy   Birth   12 Months   24 Months   36 Months   48 Months   60 Months

Source: Denboba et al. 2014.

which data are provided and analyzed. As shown in table 3.1, information in the surveys is available for 19 of the 25 interventions, including many of the most important ones. Overall, the diagnostic of the coverage of ECD interventions is thus comprehensive. An annex table provides a more complete list and definitions of indicators used for measuring coverage—and in a few cases outcomes.

Box 3.1   Essential Early Childhood Development Interventions Have High Returns

In this study, the ECD period refers to a child's growth and development starting at conception and until entry in primary school. Research suggests that interventions in the five ECD packages suggested by Denboba et al. (2014) have high returns. Examples of such high returns are as follows:

Family support package: In Africa and Asia, access to safe water can have a 3.4:1 benefit-to-cost ratio and adequate sanitation can have a 4–7:1 benefit-to-cost ratio (Rijsberman and Zwane 2012). In Africa, South America, Europe, and Southeast Asia regions, food fortification with iron and other micronutrients can have a benefit-to-cost ratio as high as 37:1 (Horton 1992). Estimates from Africa, East Asia and the Pacific, and South Asia regions indicate that salt iodization can have a benefit-to-cost ratio as high as 30:1 (Horton, Alderman, and Rivera 2008). In these same regions, vitamin A can cost US$3–16 per disability-adjusted life year saved (Ching et al. 2000; Fiedler 2000; Horton and Ross 2003).

Pregnancy package: Iron supplementation for pregnant mothers costs from $66 (African subregion with very high adult and high child mortality) – $115 (Southeast Asian subregion with high rates of adult and child mortality) per disability-adjusted life year saved (Baltussen, Knai, and Sharan 2004).

Birth package: In South Asia and Sub-Saharan Africa, a package of maternal and neonatal health packages costs $3,337–$6,129 per death averted and $92–$148 per disability-adjusted life year averted (Laxminarayan, Chow, and Shahid-Salles 2006). Breastfeeding promotion programs, which can prevent diarrhea, cost $527–$2,000 per disability-adjusted life year (ibid).

Child health and development package: Immunizations can have a benefit-to-cost ratio up to 20:1 (Barninghausen et al. 2009). In Tanzania, Zinc supplementation for diarrhea management may cost $73 per DALYs saved (Robberstad et al. 2004). Estimates from Africa, East Asia and the Pacific, and South Asia regions indicate that optimal feeding may cost $500–$1,000 per disability-adjusted life year saved (Horton et al. 2010) and deworming can have a benefit-to-cost ratio as high as 6:1 (Horton, Alderman, and Rivera 2008).

Preschool package: Increasing preschool enrollment to 50 percent of all children in low- and middle-come countries could result in lifetime earnings gains from $14–$34 billon (Engle et al. 2011). High-quality ECD programs targeting vulnerable groups in the United States have an annual rate of return of 7–16 percent (Heckman et al. 2009; Rolnick and Grunewald 2007).

Source: Denboba et al. 2014.

Table 3.1   Data Availability on Essential Interventions

Intervention	Availability in DHS
Family support package	
1. Maternal education	IDHS 2002/03, 2007, 2012
2. Planning for family size and spacing	IDHS 2002/03, 2007, 2012
3. Education about early stimulation and growth	—
4. Social assistance transfer programs	—

table continues next page

Table 3.1 Data Availability on Essential Interventions (continued)

Intervention	Availability in DHS
5. Prevention and treatment of parental depression	—
6. Parental leave and child care	—
7. Child protection services	—
8. Access to healthcare	IDHS 2002/03, 2007, 2012
9. Micronutrient supplementation and fortification	IDHS 2002/03, 2007, 2012
10. Access to safe water	IDHS 2002/03, 2007, 2012
11. Adequate sanitation	IDHS 2002/03, 2007, 2012
12. Hygiene and hand washing	IDHS 2002/03, 2007, 2012
Pregnancy package	
13. Antenatal care	IDHS 2002/03, 2007, 2012
14. Iron and folic acid for pregnant mothers	IDHS 2002/03, 2007, 2012
15. Counseling on adequate diet for pregnant mothers	IDHS 2002/03, 2007, 2012
Birth package	
16. Skilled attendance at delivery	IDHS 2002/03, 2007, 2012
17. Birth registration	IDHS 2002/03, 2007, 2012
18. Exclusive breastfeeding	IDHS 2002/03, 2007, 2012
Child health and development package	
19. Immunizations	IDHS 2002/03, 2007, 2012
20. Adequate, nutritious, and safe diet	IDHS 2002/03, 2007, 2012
21. Therapeutic zinc supplementation for diarrhea	IDHS 2002/03, 2007, 2012
22. Prevention and treatment of acute malnutrition	—
23. Deworming	IDHS 2002/03, 2007, 2012
Preschool package	
24. Preprimary education	SUSENAS 2007, 2010
25. Continuity to primary	SUSENAS and BPS Indonesia 2007, 2010

Note: BPS = *Biro Pusat Statistik* (Central Bureau of Statistics); IDHS = Indonesia Demographic and Health Survey; — = not available.

Coverage of Essential Interventions

Family Support Package

Families play a critical role in addressing children's development needs. While some ECD interventions are age specific, others are required throughout the ECD period. Denboba et al. (2014) identify 12 interventions/services in their children and families support package which are required throughout the ECD period. The interventions are (1) maternal education; (2) planning for family size and spacing; (3) education about early stimulation, growth, and development; (4) social assistance transfer programs; (5) prevention and treatment of parental depression; (6) parental leave and adequate childcare; (7) child protection services; (8) access health care; (9) micronutrients supplementation and fortification; (10) access to safe water; (11) access to sanitation; and finally (12) hygiene and hand washing. As reviewed in Denboba et al. (2014), these interventions often have high benefits. Examples of such benefits are as follows:

- A higher level of education among mothers benefits their children in multiple ways, not only for a range of health and nutrition outcomes but also for enrollment in early child care and education programs (for example, Greenberg 2011; Lombardi et al. 2014).
- Planning for family size and spacing including through contraceptive use helps parents anticipate and attain their desired number of children. Spacing improves pregnancies and deliveries and helps reduce maternal mortality (Seyfried 2011; WHO 2014).
- Support and education for parents through home visiting programs and ECD campaigns helps them learn about child health, growth, and development. This may improve feeding practices (Aboud and Akhter 2011; Bentley et al. 2010), early stimulation (Landry, Smith, and Swank, 2006; Young, 2002), and cognitive and language development (Engle et al. 2011). Child–parent interactions also enhance physical, cognitive, and socioemotional development (Grantham-McGregor et al. 2007), thereby improving future earnings (Heckman and Masterov 2007).
- Targeted transfer programs help parents provide for their children, increasing food consumption and dietary diversity (Ruel and Alderman 2013). The programs help reach vulnerable children and may improve school attendance, birth registration rates, and access to health care, while reducing child labor and violence (Barrientos et al. 2013).
- Prevention and treatment of maternal depression from pregnancy to the early years of motherhood helps reduce risks for children. Community-based interventions have been shown to reduce depressive symptoms, improve maternal sensitivity and infant attachment, infant health, and time spent playing with infants (Walker et al. 2011).
- Parental leave and child care resources help parents cater to their children (International Labour Organization 2010). They may reduce neonatal mortality, infant mortality and under-five mortality (Heymann, Raub, and Earle 2011). The programs may pay for themselves (Immervoll and Barber 2005) by increasing women's labor force participation, thereby lowing gender inequality (International Labour Organization 2010).
- Child protection services as well as positive family routines reduce risks of domestic violence affecting children's socioemotional development (Alderman 2011). Improving institutional environment of nonparental group residential care can also lead to benefits in child cognitive and social-emotional competence (Walker et al. 2011).
- Access to and affordability of health care are key for households to use the services in a preventive way, or when a child is sick or injured, thereby affecting the health and nutritional status of children (Alderman et al. 2013). Deficiencies in micronutrients such as vitamin A, iodine, iron, and zinc can cause irreversible deficits in the physical and mental development of children. Fortification of staples foods and salt iodization help prevent such deficiencies, while reducing the risk of low-birthweight babies and child mortality (Bhutta et al. 2013; Horton, Alderman, and Rivera 2008).

- Access to safe and sanitation water are essential for a range of development outcomes, including child morbidity, malnutrition, and mortality (on links between water, sanitation, and child health, see, among many others, Dillingham and Guerrant 2004; Esrey 1996; Esrey et al. 1991; Fay et al. 2005; Hutton and Haller 2004; Jalan and Ravallion 2003; Kosek, Bern, and Guerrant 2003; Moe and Rheingans 2006; Alderman et al. 2013; Bhutta, Ahmet, and Black 2008; Cairncross, Hunt, and Boisson 2010; World Bank 2010; Zwane and Kremer 2007; and Spears, 2013).
- As noted among others by Horton et al. (2010), adequate hygiene and hand washing may reduce the incidence of diarrhea by one third to half and thereby have a major impact on the health and nutrition status of children.

Table 3.1 provides data on the coverage of the various interventions in the latest available household survey, as well as changes in coverage between 2002 and 2012 (for some of the interventions discussed in this chapter, the change in coverage is computed between 2007 and 2012). Data are available for 7 of the 12 interventions. For several interventions, coverage is relatively high, at greater than 60 percent nationally. This is the case for the use of any contraceptive method, adequate treatment for acute respiratory infection, adequate treatment for fever, micronutrients (vitamin A and iron) for children, and the safe disposal of children's stools. But for some other interventions, especially key support for mothers, including the share of women who has completed at least secondary education and the share of women with health insurance offered by social security, coverage is low.

Table 3.2 also provides data on changes over time in the coverage of the interventions. For some interventions, there has been a large gain in coverage over the last decade. This is the case for adequate treatment for acute respiratory infection, adequate treatment for fever, access to improved sanitation, and the safe disposal of children's stools. For other interventions, there seems to have been a decline or stagnation in coverage rate, with the largest decline suggested for vitamin A supplement for children. There has been a decline in improved drinking water, which is a bit surprising, given the substantial gain in improved sanitation.

Finally, the table provides data on the minimum and maximum values of the indicators, as well as the changes in indicators, between provinces (the full data are available in Heejin Kim and Wodon 2014; here only summary findings are reported). Clearly, there are very large differences between provinces in the level of coverage for virtually all interventions. For all the interventions listed in table 3.2, the average gap in coverage between the least and best performing provinces is 43.7 percentage points. The largest gap is at 59.3 points for access to improved sanitation, while the smallest gap is 30.8 points for secondary education completion.

Pregnancy and Birth Packages

The second and third packages of essential interventions suggested by Denboba et al. (2014) are the pregnancy and birth packages. The pregnancy package covers the time from conception to birth while the birth package covers the time from

Table 3.2 Coverage of Interventions in the Family Support Package

Intervention	DHS indicator	National	By province Min	Max
Coverage in 2012				
1. Maternal education	Female education (secondary completion)	23.4	13.0	43.8
2. Family planning and spacing	Use of any contraceptive method	61.9	21.8	70.3
	Use of any modern contraceptive method	57.9	19.1	66.4
	Media exposure to family planning messages	45.3	17.7	72.9
8. Access to health care	Female health insurance coverage	25.7	7.2	60.7
	Problem in accessing health care	34.1	25.7	64.0
	Adequate treatment for acute respiratory illness	75.3	53.7	100.0
	Adequate treatment for fever	73.5	52.0	84.1
9. Micronutrients	Vitamin A supplement for children	61.1	32.0	74.7
	Consumed foods rich in iron for children	67.5	50.8	78.3
10. Access to safe water	Access to improved drinking water	41.1	17.8	58.6
11. Adequate sanitation	Access to improved sanitation	57.8	25.1	84.4
12. Hygiene and hand washing	Hand washing	34.6	11.9	49.0
	Safe disposal of children's stools	79.7	34.2	94.7
Change in coverage (2002–12, unless indicated otherwise)				
1. Maternal education	Female education (secondary completion)	7.6	4.1	15.2
2. Planning for family size and spacing	Use of any contraceptive method	1.6	−5.9	13.1
	Use of any modern contraceptive method	1.2	-4.0	13.3
	Media exposure to family planning messages	−2.7	−36.4	25.3
8. Access to health care	Female health insurance coverage	—	—	—
	Problem in accessing health care	−2.0	−21.1	29.2
	Adequate treatment for acute respiratory illness	18.5	−7.0	38.6
	Adequate treatment for fever	16.7	−12.4	27.2
9. Micronutrients	Vitamin A supplement for children	−14	−28.9	7.1
	Consumed foods rich in iron for children[a]	−2.2	−25.3	10.8
10. Access to safe water	Access to improved drinking water	−6.6	−39.6	36.5
11. Adequate sanitation	Access to improved sanitation	22.2	7.1	34.8
12. Hygiene and hand washing	Hand washing	—	—	—
	Safe disposal of children's stools	13.3	-4.4	31.6

Source: 2012 IDHS.
a. Change over time is measured between 2007 and 2012. — = not available.

birth to six months of age. Each of the two packages includes three main interventions. The combined six interventions, numbered 13–18, are (13) antenatal visits; (14) iron and folic acid for pregnant mothers; (15) counseling on adequate diet during pregnancy; (16) attended delivery; (17) birth registration; and (18) exclusive breastfeeding. Again, these various interventions tend to have high benefits and thereby also high returns. Examples of such benefits/returns are as follows:

- Antenatal visits: These visits provide opportunities for health care providers to deliver a package of services including screening tests, counseling on reduced workload, treatment for identified complications, and behavior-change communication to increase women's skills in identifying danger signs and potential complications. The United Nations Children's Fund (UNICEF) and World Health Organization (WHO) recommend a minimum of four antenatal care visits during pregnancy. Parenting education for expectant mothers is also important to cater future mothers with key parenting skills to improve outcomes for newborns. Antenatal visits reduce the risk of maternal and neonatal death (UNICEF 2009).
- Iron and folic acid for pregnant mothers: Nearly one-quarter of maternal deaths are caused by hemorrhages, which are closely linked to anemia during pregnancy (Black, Victora, and Walker 2013). Iron and folic acid supplementation for pregnant women can reduce anemia as well as the risk of low-birthweight babies.
- Counseling on adequate diets for pregnant mothers: Undernutrition during pregnancy can affect fetal growth and development. An estimated 800,000 newborn deaths each year can be attributed to the increased risk associated with fetal growth restriction (Black, Victora, and Walker 2013). Counseling women on healthy diets and lifestyles during pregnancy can help to ensure that they have an adequate diet, including nutrient-rich food.
- Skilled attendants at delivery: Most of the direct causes of maternal mortality related to obstetric complications can be addressed if skilled health personnel are present during delivery and referral facilities are available. Skilled attended delivery can address the risks of birth defects and maternal mortality.
- Birth registration: Worldwide, as many as one in three children younger than five years of age are not currently registered (UNICEF 2012). Birth registration is a first step to reach children with the services they need to fully develop. Some form of birth registration is generally required for children to obtain a birth certificate and access to services, protection and opportunities throughout life.
- Exclusive breastfeeding: Following early initiation of breastfeeding within one hour of birth, exclusive breastfeeding for the first six months contributes to a child's short- and long-term health and development through the provision of rich nutritional inputs and positive socioemotional interaction between mother and child (Nelson 2007), as well as avoiding diseases caused by contact with contaminated food or water. Promotion of exclusive breastfeeding is

one of the most promising interventions for improving child survival in the first six months of life.

Table 3.3 provides the data on coverage levels and changes in coverage over time. Data are available for all six interventions. Coverage tends to be higher for many of these interventions than was the case for the family support package, reaching 95.7 percent in the case of antenatal care.[1] The lowest coverage rates, all at just below or above half of the population being covered, are for consultations in the case of pregnancy complications, vitamin A supplements during pregnancy, counseling on diet during the pregnancy, birth registration, and breastfeeding within the first hour. In terms of changes over time in coverage,

Table 3.3 Coverage of Interventions in the Pregnancy and Birth Packages

Intervention	DHS indicator	National	Min	Max
Coverage in 2012				
13. Antenatal care	Antenatal care	95.7	57.8	99.3
	Consultation on pregnancy complications	53.0	27.9	66.5
14. Iron and folic acid for pregnancy	Vitamin A supplement for pregnancy	48.1	29.7	60.7
	Iron for pregnant mothers	75.5	31.9	96.6
15. Counseling on diet for pregnancy	Counseling on diet for pregnancy	52.8	21.8	76.3
16. Skilled attendance at delivery	Delivery attended by skilled personnel	83.1	39.9	98.7
	Delivery in a health facility	63.2	16.7	98.4
17. Birth registration	Birth registration	47.7	20.2	82.0
18. Exclusive breastfeeding	Breastfeeding within the first hour	49.3	17.1	73.7
Change in coverage (2002–12, unless indicated otherwise)				
13. Antenatal care	Antenatal care	4.2	−1.7	21.9
	Consultation on pregnancy complications	24.3	−1.6	39.9
14. Iron and folic acid for pregnancy	Vitamin A supplement for pregnancy	5.6	−10.9	23.3
	Iron for pregnant mothers	−2.9	−20.1	14.2
15. Counseling on diet for pregnancy	Counseling on diet for pregnancy	17.8	−36.7	39.0
16. Skilled attendance at delivery	Delivery attended by skilled personnel	16.8	0.1	31.6
	Delivery in a health facility	23.5	4.3	47.1
17. Birth registration	Birth registration	3.6	−21.0	23.0
18. Exclusive breastfeeding	Breastfeeding within the first hour	10.6	−20.3	41.1

Source: 2012 IDHS.

Early Childhood Education and Development in Indonesia • http://dx.doi.org/10.1596/978-1-4648-0646-9

there have been gains for all interventions except for iron for pregnant mothers. In some cases the gains have been large (above 20 points) and in other cases smaller. But as for the family support package, there are again large differences between provinces in coverage. For all the interventions listed in table 3.3, the average gap in coverage between the least and best performing provinces is 54.3 percentage points. The largest gap is at 81.7 points for delivery in a health facility, and the smallest is at 31.0 points for vitamin A supplement during the pregnancy.

Child Health and Development

The fourth package of essential services is the child health and development package which covers the time from birth to six years of age. The main risks of not providing essential services during this period are stunted growth, anemia, impaired cognitive development, and child mortality. The package consists of six main interventions or services numbered 19–23: (19) immunizations; (20) adequate, nutritious, and safe diet; (21) therapeutic zinc supplementation for diarrhea; (22) prevention and treatment of acute malnutrition; and (23) deworming. Examples of such benefits or returns mentioned by Denboba et al. (2014) are as follows:

- Immunizations: Starting at birth, a complete course of childhood immunizations is essential in reducing child morbidity and mortality. According to the WHO, increasing coverage of PCV, Rota, and Hib vaccine could have prevented 1.5 million deaths of children younger than five years of age in 2002 (Barnighausen et al. 2009). According to the Copenhagen Consensus, expanded immunization coverage for children is among the top ten most productive investments for countries.
- Adequate, nutritious, and safe diet: After six months of exclusive breastfeeding, mothers should continue to breastfeed through 24 months while providing complementary feeding with age-appropriate amounts, frequency, consistency, and variety of safely prepared foods. Responsive feeding practices are important, as is adequate feeding during and after illness. After two years, young children continue to need adequate, nutritious, and safe diets. Undernutrition leads to weakened immune systems of babies and young children, putting them at a greater risk of falling sick from preventable illnesses like pneumonia and diarrhea. Nearly one-fifth of deaths of children younger than five years of age could be prevented with optimal feeding (UNICEF 2009).
- Therapeutic zinc supplementation for diarrhea: Approximately 1.5 million children in the developing world die from diarrhea each year. Therapeutic zinc supplementation can reduce deaths from diarrhea by almost one quarter (UNICEF 2009).
- Prevention and treatment of acute malnutrition: Proven interventions include complementary and therapeutic feeding to provide micronutrient-fortified and/ or enhanced complementary foods for the prevention and treatment of moderate malnutrition among children 6–23 months of age and community-based

management of severe acute malnutrition among children younger than five years of age. Community-based management of acute malnutrition includes (a) in-patient care for children with severe acute malnutrition with medical complications and infants younger than six months of age with visible signs of severe acute malnutrition; (b) out-patient care for children with severe acute malnutrition without medical complications; and (c) community outreach (Horton et al. 2010).

- Deworming: Worm infections are a chronic condition that affect children's health, nutrition, and development and, as a consequence, limit their ability to access and benefit from education. Worms can cause children to become anemic and malnourished and can impair their mental and physical development (Hotez et al. 2006). Deworming is simple, safe, and inexpensive and has beneficial effects on educational outcomes.

Table 3.4 provides the data on coverage levels and changes in coverage over time. Data are available for all five interventions. For a few interventions, coverage is again relatively high, at above 60 percent nationally, although this is still not high enough for relatively simple interventions such as immunizations. The lowest coverage rate is for deworming medication for children, at only a quarter of the target group covered. In terms of changes over time in coverage, there have been gains for all interventions for which data are available, which is good news even though some of the gains are small in comparison to the remaining gaps. In

Table 3.4 Coverage of Child Health and Development Interventions

Intervention	DHS indicator	National	Min	Max
Coverage in 2012				
19. Immunizations	Immunization (DPT3)	72.0	35.3	96.4
	Immunization (measles)	80.1	49.0	97.1
20. Adequate, nutritious, and safe diet	Adequate diet for children	36.6	16.3	55.5
21. Therapeutic zinc supplementationfor diarrhea	Adequate treatment for diarrhea	64.6	45.3	81.6
	Oral rehydration therapy for diarrhea	46.8	31.4	73.3
23. Deworming	Deworming medication for children	25.9	6.6	34.8
Change in coverage (2002–12, unless indicated otherwise)				
19. Immunizations	Immunization (DPT3)	13.7	−4.4	26.1
	Immunization (measles)	8.5	−5.9	17.4
20. Adequate, nutritious, and safe diet	Adequate diet for children[a]	−4.6	−24.4	13.0
21. Therapeutic zinc supplementationfor diarrhea	Adequate treatment for diarrhea	16.8	−24.7	39.1
	Oral rehydration therapy for diarrhea	8.5	−4.7	36.1
23. Deworming	Deworming medication for children	—	—	—

Source: 2012 IDHS.
Note: DPT = diphtheria, pertussis, and tetanus.
a. Change over time is measured between 2007 and 2012.

terms of differences between provinces, the average gap in coverage between the least and best performing provinces is 42.5 percentage points, with the largest gap observed for immunization (DPT3) at 61.1 points and the smallest gap observed for deworming medication for children at 28.2 points, in part because coverage remains relatively low for all provinces for that intervention.

Schooling Interventions

The last and fifth package of essential ECD interventions outlined by Denboba et al. (2014) is the preschool package, which covers the period from three to six years of age. The quality of a child's early learning experience makes a significant difference to school preparation, participation, completion, and achievement. Without adequate early childhood education, young children may not have the necessary skills to fully benefit from the education they receive at the primary level. The preschool package consists of two interventions/services, which, given the interventions, are numbered 24 and 25, (24) early childhood and preprimary programs, and (25) continuity to quality primary education. As reviewed in Denboba et al. (2014), and as was the case for other interventions reviewed in this chapter, these two interventions tend to have high benefits/returns. Examples are as follows:

- Preprimary education: Young children need sustained access to supportive, nurturing environments that provide a high degree of cognitive stimulation and emotional care throughout the early years (UNESCO 2014). Compared to children who attend quality preprimary programs, children who enter school without adequate preparation are more likely to have poor academic performance, repeat grades, and drop out of school (Currie and Thomas 1999; Feinstein, 2003; Heckman and Masterov 2007; Reynolds et al. 2001). Beyond access, quality in preprimary education is equally critical. Children will only benefit from increased access to early childhood care and education (ECCE) if the services provided meet core quality standards. Quality preprimary programs are linked to lifelong benefits for individuals and society at large. They reduce the need for remedial education or rehabilitative actions later on, including in terms of reducing the risk of incarceration and improving welfare in adulthood (Schweinhart et al. 2005).
- Continuity to primary school: During the period of time when children move from either home or an early childhood program into primary school, they experience demanding changes (Arnold et al. 2006; Fabian and Dunlop 2007). For the transition to be smooth, children need to be ready for school and, equally important, schools need to be ready for children (Consultative Group on EECD 1991; Myers and Landers 1989). Evidence suggests that the failure of the first year or two of school to establish basic literacy skills creates inefficiencies that reverberate through a child's progression through the education system (Abadzi 2006). Young children should possess the school readiness skills necessary—physical health and well-being, social

Table 3.5 Coverage of Education Interventions

Intervention	DHS indicator	National	Min	Max
Coverage in 2012				
24. Preprimary education	Net enrollment rate in preprimary education (ages 3–4 years)	15.3	3.6	45.2
	Net enrollment rate in preprimary education (ages 5–6 years)	32.6	7.5	74.8
25. Continuity to primary	Net enrollment rate in primary education (ages 7–12 years)	92.5	70.8	96.0
Change in coverage (2002–12, unless indicated otherwise)				
24. Preprimary education	Net enrollment rate in preprimary education (ages 3–4 years)[a]	5.3	−3.4	21.9
	Net enrollment rate in preprimary education (ages 5–6 years)[a]	14.7	−0.9	35.9
25. Continuity to primary	Net enrollment rate in primary education (ages 7–12 years)[a]	−1.3	−10.2	2.6

Source: SUSENAS 2007, 2012 databases and BPS Indonesia Statistics.
a. Change over time is measured between 2007 and 2012.

competence, emotional maturity, language and cognitive development, communication skills, and general knowledge—to be able to learn effectively in school (Janus and Offord 2000). Ensuring continuity between early childhood and primary years is important to counter potential fade-out of the impact of preschools in primary school. Quality improvement in early primary grades (integrating ECCE/early primary experience, teacher training on classroom strategies for young children, and smaller class size) can improve learning outcomes, school attendance, pass rates, and promotions and reduce dropout and repetition rates (Arnold et al. 2008). Well-trained and high-quality experienced teachers in the early grades of primary school can help close the readiness gaps that young children may face (Pianta, Laparo, and Hamre 2007; Schady et al. 2014).

Table 3.5 provides the data on coverage levels and changes in coverage over time. Data are available for both interventions. Enrollment rates are very low for preschools, whether one considers the age group of three and four years or that of children five or six years old, although as was to be expected, coverage is higher for the older age group. By contrast, net enrollment rates in primary school are high. In terms of changes over time in coverage, there has been a substantial gain for preschool enrollment which has nearly doubled between 2007 and 2012, but the net enrollment rate in primary school has decreased. This may however not necessarily be a negative outcome if it denotes that fewer students are too old for their grade. As always, the differences between provinces are large, with the average gap in coverage between the least and best performing provinces being at 44.7 percentage points for the three interventions listed, and larger than that for preschool enrolment among five- or six-year-olds.

Comparing Coverage Rates and Changes in Coverage Rates
Figures 3.2 and 3.3 provide a visual summary of the data on coverage and changes in coverage over time. In figure 3.2, interventions are ranked by level of

Figure 3.2   Coverage of Essential Early Childhood Development Interventions, 2012

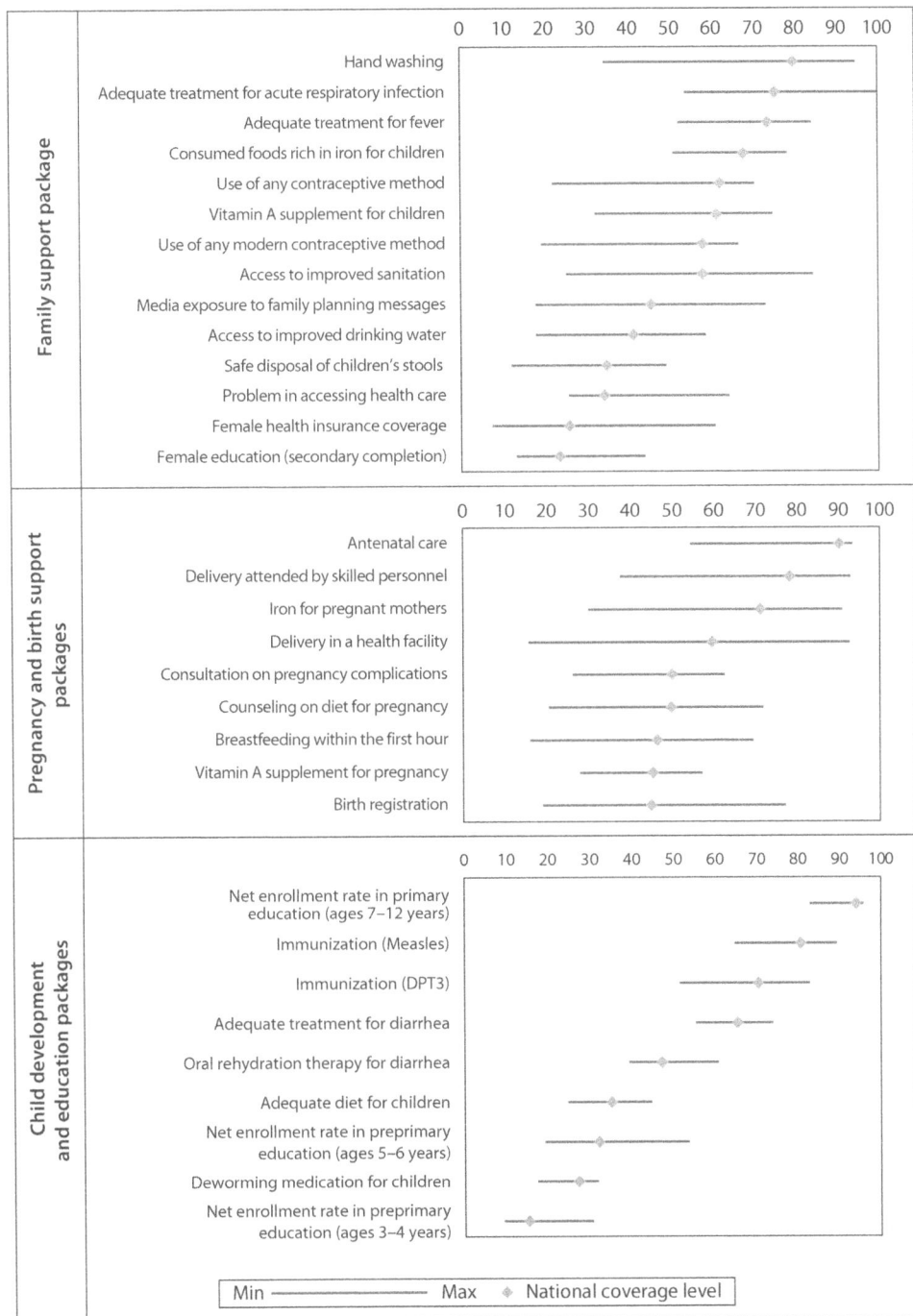

Source: 2012 IDHS.

Figure 3.3 Change in Coverage over Time (2002–12, Unless Indicated Otherwise)

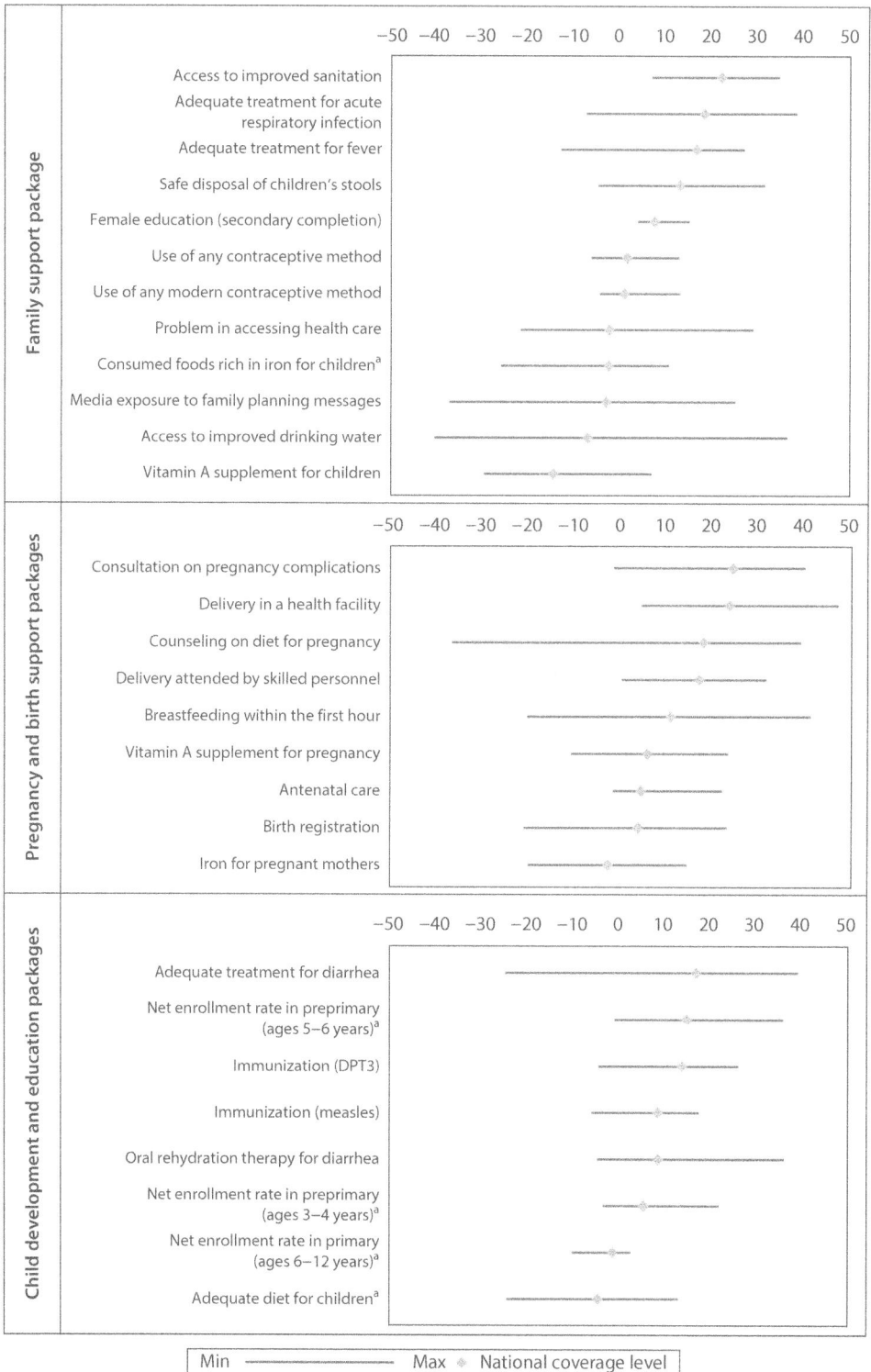

Source: 2002/03, 2007 and 2012 IDHS.
a. Change over time is measured between 2007 and 2012.

coverage from the intervention with the most coverage to that with the least coverage. In figure 3.3, the same principle is applied, but the ranking is based on the size of the change in coverage. In both figures, the red dot represents the national coverage level, while the blue bar represents the difference between the least and best performing provinces for each indicator. Together the two figures provide a simple diagnostic of the level of coverage for the various types of interventions, and the improvements in coverage over time or lack thereof, depending on the indicators.

Figure 3.2 underscores again the fact that there are today large differences in the coverage of various interventions, often with a gap of up to 50 percentage points between the provices with the lowest coverage and the provinces with the highest coverage. Figure 3.3 shows that it is not necessarily a given for coverage to increase over time. For some interventions, there has been a decline in coverage between the various survey years. Some of this may be related to differences in survey coverage between years. In addition, it should be kept in mind that all estimates are based on survey data, so that the estimates have standard errors, and these are larger at the level of individual provinces than at the level of the country as a whole, given the smaller sample size at the level of individual provinces. But at the same time, there is also evidence of losses in coverage for some intervntions, including at the national level. This is more the case for interventions in the family support package than for the interventions in other opackages. A more detailed analysis of changes in coverage over time is available in a companion piece by Heejin Kim and Wodon (2015).

Coverage and Level of Economic Development

This last section provides a brief analysis of the relationship between the level of economic development of provinces and the coverage of the essential interventions. One would expect a positive relationship, but also substantial variability, with some poorer provinces at times performing better than richer ones. The extent to which the relationship between the coverage of interventions and the level of economic development is strong can be measured through the R^2 value associated with a regression line through the scatter plot of coverage rates as a function of provincial gross domestic product (GDP) per capita. This can be done for each intervention separately.

The results are displayed in table 3.6. Figure 3.4 ranks the intervention according to the strength of those relationships. In general, the relationships are not very strong, suggesting that comparatively high coverage can be achieved even in provinces with low levels of GDP per capita. The highest R^2 value is observed for the share of women who have completed secondary education, with GDP per capita explaining 44.5 percent of the variation in coverage. The lowest R^2 value is vitamin A supplement for children, use of any modern contraceptive method, and enrollment in primary education, which present virtually zero relationship (R^2 values less than 0.100). In other words,

Figure 3.4   Coverage of Early Childhood Development Interventions and Economic Development

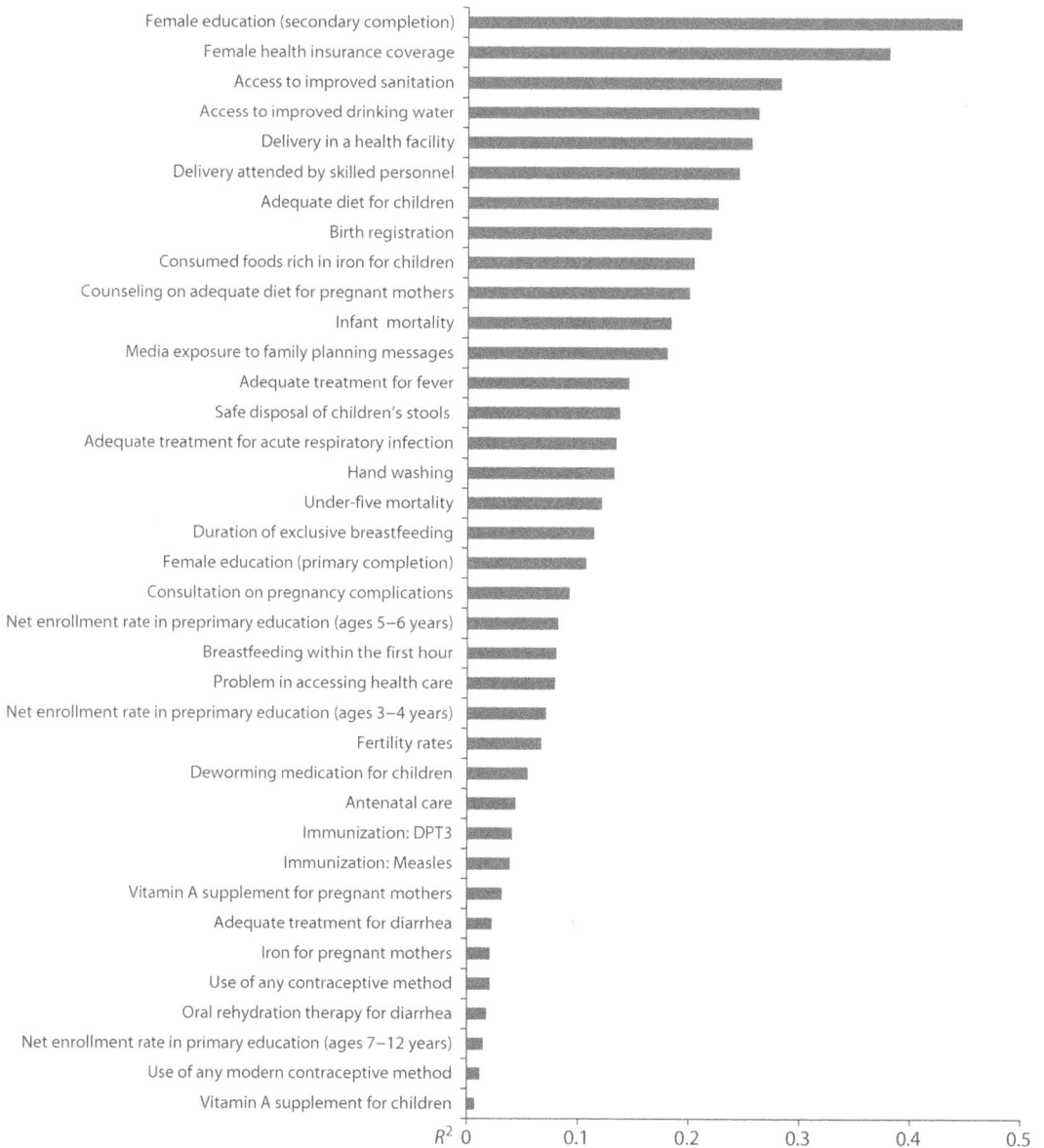

Source: 2012 IDHS.

provinces and the country as a whole cannot rely on economic growth to somehow lift up the coverage of the various interventions in a systematic way—specific policies and programs are required to increase coverage rates. This is also observed in figure 3.5, which displays the R^2 values for the relationship between changes in GDP and change in coverage. These R^2 values are typically smaller in differences than is the case in levels.

Figure 3.5   Changes in Coverage of Early Childhood Development Intervention and Change in Economic Development (2002–12, Unless Indicated Otherwise)

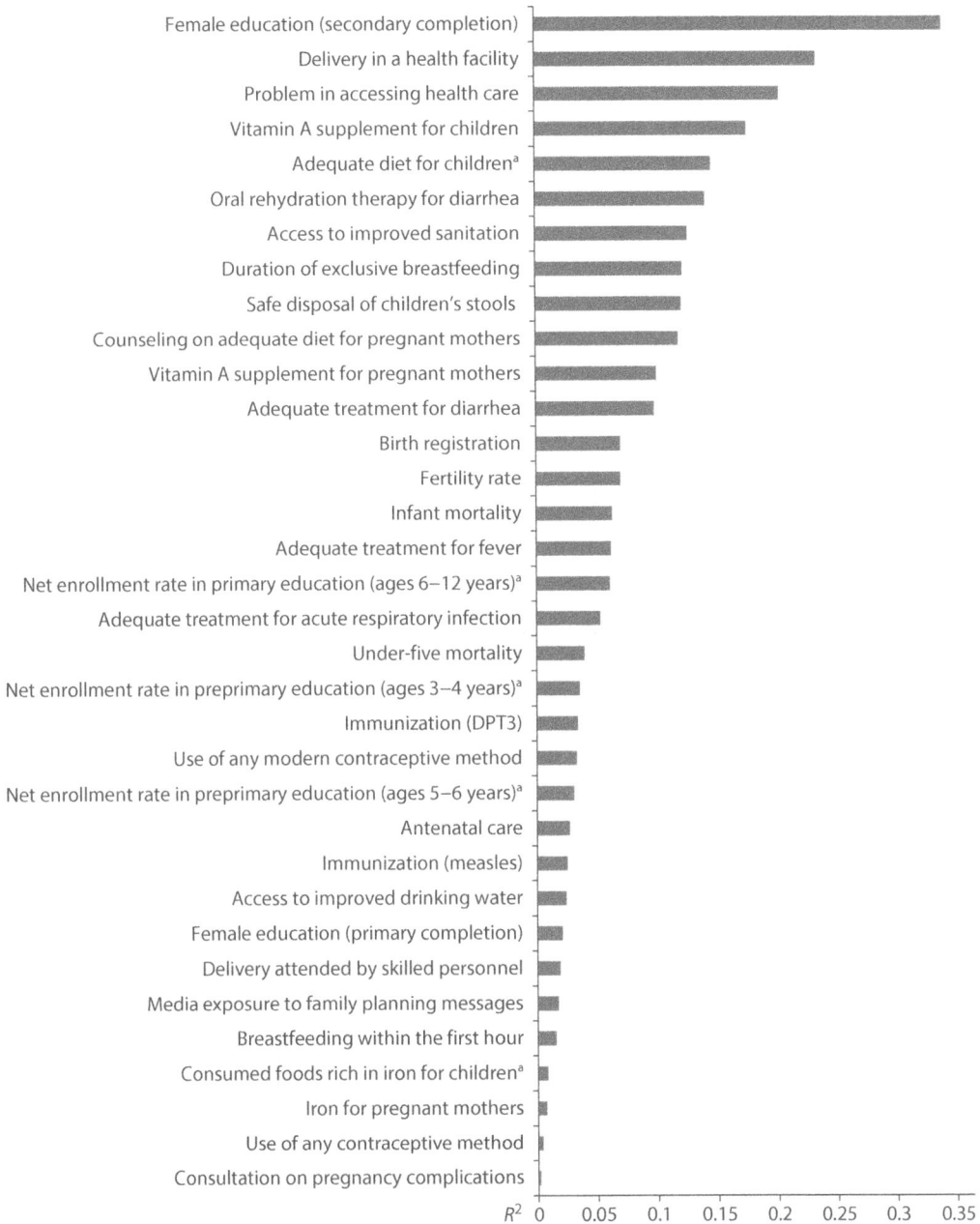

Source: 2002/03, 2007, and 2012 IDHS and BPS Indonesia.
a. Change over time is measured between 2007 and 2012.

Conclusion

In the SABER-ECD framework, the second policy goal refers to the extent to which policies and programs are implemented widely—in terms of scope, coverage, and equity. The objective of this chapter was to document in more details the coverage of essential ECD interventions with a focus on differences between provinces. The analysis focused on 25 essential interventions for young children grouped into five packages: the pregnancy, birth, child health, preschool, and family support packages. Information was available in the surveys for 19 of the 25 interventions considered, so the diagnostic provided was fairly comprehensive.

The diagnostic suggests major disparities in coverage between provinces. On average, across provinces, some services such as entry in primary school, antenatal care, access to health care have high coverage, while others such as maternal education (at least secondary), preprimary education, birth registration have low coverage. But the averages mask very large coverage differentials between provinces, often at 40–50 percentage points per intervention.

Note

1. Antenatal care refers to the percentage of women ages 15–49 years who had a live birth in the five years receiving antenatal care (four visits) from a skilled provider (doctor, obstetrician, nurse, midwife, and village midwife) for the most recent birth. However, this figure does not consider the timing of antenatal checks as recommended by WHO (1–2 visits at first, second, and third trimesters, respectively). The Basic Health Profile 2013 (RISKESDAS 2013) indicates that the national average of the antenatal check that takes into consideration the timing of antenatal checks was 70.4 percent.

Annex 3A

Table 3A.1 Description of Indicators Used to Measure Coverage

Intervention	DHS indicator	Description
1. Maternal education	Female education (primary/ secondary completion)	Percent distribution of women ages 15–49 years, by highest level of schooling completed Primary completion: completed sixth grade at the primary level Secondary completion: completed sixth grade at the secondary level
2. Planning for family size and spacing	Fertility rates	Total fertility rate, the percentage of women ages 15–49 years who are currently pregnant, and the mean number of children ever born to women ages 40–49 years
	Use of any contraceptive method	Percent distribution of currently married women ages 15–49 years by contraceptive method currently used Any traditional method: rhythm, withdrawal, other Any modern method: female sterilization, male sterilization, pill, intrauterine device, injectable, implants, male condom, diaphragm (intravag), lactational amenorrhea, emergency contraception
	Media exposure to family planning messages	Percentage of currently married women ages 15–49 years who heard or saw a family planning message on television in the past few months
8. Access to healthcare	Infant/under-five mortality	Total number of deaths per 1,000 live births Infant mortality: the probability of dying between birth and exactly age one year Under-five mortality: the probability of dying between birth and exactly age five years
	Female health insurance coverage	Percentage of women ages 15–49 years with health insurance coverage offered by social security
	Problem in accessing health care	Percentage of women ages 15–49 years who reported that they have serious problems in accessing health care for themselves when they are sick
	Adequate treatment for acute respiratory infection	Among children younger than five years of age, the percentage who had symptoms of acute respiratory infection in the two weeks preceding the survey and among children with symptoms of acute respiratory infection, the percentage for whom advice or treatment was sought from a health facility or provider
	Adequate treatment for fever	Among children younger than five years of age, the percentage who had a fever in the two weeks preceding the survey; and among children with fever, the percentage for whom advice or treatment was sought from a health facility or provider
9. Micronutrient supplementation and fortification	Vitamin A supplement for children	Among all children 6–59 months, the percentages who were given vitamin A supplements in the six months preceding the survey
	Consumed foods rich in iron for children	Among youngest children ages 6–23 months who are living with their mother, the percentages who consumed iron-rich foods in the day or night preceding the survey

table continues next page

Table 3A.1 Description of Indicators Used to Measure Coverage (*continued*)

Intervention	DHS indicator	Description
10. Access to safe water	Access to improved drinking water	Percent distribution of households and de jure population with improved source of drinking water
11. Adequate sanitation	Access to improved sanitation	Percent distribution of households and de jure population having improved with improved sanitation facilities
12. Hygiene and hand washing	Hand washing	Percentage of households in which the place for hand washing was observed
	Safe disposal of children's stools	Percent distribution of youngest children younger than five years of age living with the mother by the manner of disposal of the child's last fecal matter, and percentage of children whose stools are disposed of safely using toilet/latrine
13. Antenatal care	Antenatal care	Percentage of women ages 15–49 years who had a live birth in the five years receiving antenatal care from a skilled provider (doctor, obstetrician, nurse, midwife, and village midwife) for the most recent birth
	Consultation on pregnancy complications	Among women ages 15–49 years who received antenatal care for their most recent birth in the past five years, the percentage of women who informed of sings of pregnancy complications
14. Iron and folic acid for pregnant mothers	Iron for pregnant mothers	Among women with a live birth in the past five years, the percentage who took iron tablets or syrup during the pregnancy of their last birth
15. Counseling on adequate diet for pregnant mothers	Counseling on adequate diet for pregnant mothers	Percentage of last births in the two years preceding the survey whose father discussed with a health care provider about the type of foods the mother eats during pregnancy
16. Skilled attendance at delivery	Delivery attended by skilled personnel	Percentage of live births in the five years preceding the survey assisted by a skilled provider (doctor, obstetrician, nurse, midwife, and village midwife)
	Delivery in a health facility	Percentage of live births in the five years preceding the survey who delivered in a health facility
17. Birth registration	Birth registration	Percentage of the de jure population younger than five years of age whose births are registered with the civil authorities
18. Exclusive breast-feeding	Breastfeeding within the first hour	Among last-born children who were born in the two years preceding the survey, the percentages who started breastfeeding within one hour
	Duration of exclusive breast-feeding	Median duration of exclusive breastfeeding among children born in the three years preceding the survey
19. Immunizations	Immunization (DPT3/measles)	Percentage of children age 12–23 months who received specific vaccines at any time before the survey, according to a vaccination card and the mother's report

table continues next page

Table 3A.1 Description of Indicators Used to Measure Coverage (*continued*)

Intervention	DHS indicator	Description
20. Adequate, nutritious, and safe diet	Adequate diet for children	Among all children age 6–23 months living with their mother, percentage of youngest children who are fed according to three infant and young child feeding feeding practices, including timely initiation of feeding solid/semisolid foods from age 6 months, feeding small amounts, and increasing the amount of foods and frequency of feeding as the child gets older, while maintaining frequent breastfeeding
21. Therapeutic zinc supplementation for diarrhea	Adequate treatment for diarrhea	Among children younger than five years of age who had diarrhea in the two weeks preceding the survey, the percentage for whom advice or treatment was sought from a health facility or provider
	Oral rehydration therapy for diarrhea	Among children younger than five years of age who had diarrhea in the two weeks preceding the survey, the percentage given oral rehydration therapy, including fluid from oral rehydration salts packets or prepackaged liquid or recommended home fluids
23. Deworming	Deworming medication for children	Among youngest children age 6–23 months who are living with their mother, the percentages who were given deworming medication in the six months preceding the survey
24. Preprimary education	Net enrollment rate in preprimary education	The number of children enrolled in preprimary school who belong to the age group that officially corresponds to preprimary schooling, divided by the total population of the same age group
25. Continuity to primary	Net enrollment rate in primary education	The number of children enrolled in primary school who belong to the age group that officially corresponds to primary schooling, divided by the total population of the same age group

Source: IDHS and SUSENAS surveys.
Note: DPT = diphtheria, pertussis, and tetanus.

Table A.2   Relation between Coverage Levels and Economic Development

Intervention	DHS indicator	R^2
1. Maternal education	Female education (primary completion)	0.107
1. Maternal education	Female education (secondary completion)	0.445
2. Planning for family size and spacing	Fertility rates	0.067
	Use of any contraceptive method	0.021
	Use of any modern contraceptive method	0.012
	Media exposure to family planning messages	0.180
8. Access to healthcare	Infant mortality	0.183
	Under-five mortality	0.121
	Female health insurance coverage	0.380
	Problem in accessing health care	0.079
	Adequate treatment for acute respiratory infection	0.134
	Adequate treatment for fever	0.145
9. Micronutrient supplementation and fortification	Vitamin A supplement for children	0.007
	Consumed foods rich in iron for children	0.204
10. Access to safe water	Access to improved drinking water	0.262
11. Adequate sanitation	Access to improved sanitation	0.282
12. Hygiene and hand washing	Hand washing	0.132
	Safe disposal of children's stools	0.137
13. Antenatal care	Antenatal care	0.044
	Consultation on pregnancy complications	0.092
14. Iron and folic acid for pregnant mothers	Vitamin A supplement for pregnant mothers	0.032
	Iron for pregnant mothers	0.021
15. Counseling on diet for pregnancy	Counseling on adequate diet for pregnant mothers	0.200
16. Skilled attendance at delivery	Delivery attended by skilled personnel	0.245
	Delivery in a health facility	0.256
17. Birth registration	Birth registration	0.220
18. Exclusive breastfeeding	Breastfeeding within the first hour	0.080
	Duration of exclusive breastfeeding	0.114
19. Immunizations	Immunization (DPT3)	0.041
	Immunization (measles)	0.039
20. Adequate, nutritious, and safe diet	Adequate diet for children	0.226
21. Therapeutic zinc supplementation for diarrhea	Adequate treatment for diarrhea	0.023
	Oral rehydration therapy for diarrhea	0.018
23. Deworming	Deworming medication for children	0.055
24. Preprimary education	Net enrollment rate in preprimary education (age 3–4)	0.071
	Net enrollment rate in preprimary education (age 5–6)	0.082
25. Continuity to primary	Net enrollment rate in primary education (age 7–12)	0.015
Highest R^2	Female education (secondary completion)	0.445
Lowest R^2	Vitamin A supplement for children	0.007

Source: 2012 IDHS and BPS Indonesia.
Note: DPT = diphtheria, pertussis, and tetanus.

Table A.3 Relation between Change in Coverage Levels and Change in Economic Development

Intervention	DHS indicator	R^2
1. Maternal education	Female education (primary completion)	0.021
	Female education (secondary completion)	0.338
2. Planning for family size and spacing	Fertility rates	0.070
	Use of any contraceptive method	0.004
	Use of any modern contraceptive method	0.033
	Media exposure to family planning messages	0.017
8. Access to healthcare	Infant mortality	0.063
	Under-five mortality	0.040
	Problem in accessing health care	0.202
	Adequate treatment for acute respiratory infection	0.053
	Adequate treatment for fever	0.062
9. Micronutrient supplementation and fortification	Vitamin A supplement for children	0.175
	Consumed foods rich in iron for children[a]	0.008
10. Access to safe water	Access to improved drinking water	0.024
11. Adequate sanitation	Access to improved sanitation	0.126
12. Hygiene and hand washing	Safe disposal of children's stools	0.121
13. Antenatal care	Antenatal care	0.027
	Consultation on pregnancy complications	0.002
14. Iron and folic acid for pregnant mothers	Vitamin A supplement for pregnant mothers	0.100
	Iron for pregnant mothers	0.007
15. Counseling on diet for pregnancy	Counseling on adequate diet for pregnant mothers	0.118
16. Skilled attendance at delivery	Delivery attended by skilled personnel	0.019
	Delivery in a health facility	0.233
17. Birth registration	Birth registration	0.070
18. Exclusive breastfeeding	Breastfeeding within the first hour	0.015
	Duration of exclusive breastfeeding	0.122
19. Immunizations	Immunization (DPT3)	0.034
	Immunization (measles)	0.025
20. Adequate, nutritious, and safe diet	Adequate diet for children[a]	0.146
21. Therapeutic zinc supplementation for diarrhea	Adequate treatment for diarrhea	0.098
	Oral rehydration therapy for diarrhea	0.141
24. Preprimary education	Net enrollment rate in preprimary education (ages 3–4 years)[a]	0.036
	Net enrollment rate in preprimary education (ages 5–6 years)[a]	0.031
25. Continuity to primary	Net enrollment rate in primary education (ages 7–12 years)[a]	0.061
Highest R^2	Female education (secondary completion)	0.338
Lowest R^2	Consultation on pregnancy complications	0.002

Source: 2002/03, 2007, and 2012 IDHS and BPS Indonesia.
a. Change over time is measured between 2007 and 2012. DPT = diphtheria, pertussis, and tetanus.

CHAPTER 4

District-Level SABER-ECD Assessments

Lindsay Adams, Amina Denboba, Rebecca Sayre, Titie Hadiyati,
Djoko Hartono, Janice Heejin Kim, Amer Hasan, Rosfita Roesli,
Mayla Safuro, and Quentin Wodon

Abstract

In chapter 2, the Systems Approach for Better Education Results-Early Childhood Development (SABER-ECD) tool was applied at the national level for Indonesia. But substantial decentralization has taken place, with districts now being in charge of the implementation of a number of policies and programs related to early childhood development (ECD). It is therefore useful to also look at the results of the implementation of SABER-ECD tool at the district level. This is done in this chapter for five illustrative districts in order to document differences in policies and programs between districts.

Introduction

While assessing ECD policies at the national level is very important, it may not be sufficient, given that substantial decentralization leads to many decisions being made at lower administrative levels instead of centrally. In Indonesia, districts have a key role in the implementation of ECD programs and policies. It is therefore useful to also look at the results of the implementation of SABER-ECD tool at the district level. This cannot be done for all districts as part of this study, given that there over 400 of of them. But it can be done for a few districts as illustrative cases of potential differences in policies and programs between districts. The districts focused on in this chapter were selected in consultation with Bappenas to reflect a range of implementation arrangements and capacity.

For this chapter, data were collected in five districts or regencies: Kapuas in Central Kalimantan Province, Manggarai Timur in East Nusa Tenggara province, Pacitan in East Java Province, Sukabumi in West Java Province, and Sumbawa in West Nusa Tenggara Province. Data at the district level on economic development tend not to be available, but data are available at the provincial level. As shown in table 4.1, to the extent that the various districts are illustrative of the

Table 4.1 Basic Statistics at Provincial Level

Province (district)	Provincial population at 2010 Census	Provincial area (km²)	Provincial population density per km²	GDP per capita (PPP, current international $)
Provinces with one of the five districts				
East Java (Pacitan)	37,476,757	47,799	828	10051.6
West Java (Sukabumi)	43,053,732	35,377	1176	7917.0
Central Kalimantan (Kapuas)	2,212,089	153,564	14	9257.7
West Nusa Tenggara (Sumbawa)	4,500,212	18,572	234	4434.9
East Nusa Tenggara (Manggarai Timur)	4,683,827	48,718	92	2877.7
Country average	—	—	—	**9558.8**

Source: Based on the 2012 DHS report, BPS-Statistics Indonesia, and the World Development Database.
Note: GDP = gross domestic product; PPP = purchasing power parity; — = not applicable.

standards of living in their broader province, two of the districts, Pacitan and Kapuas, tend to be relatively well off, while Sukabumi is located in a province with an average level of gross domestic product (GDP) per capita. The last two districts, Manggarai Timur and Sumbawa, are located in poorer provinces. One would then expect—and this is indeed observed—that levels of coverage of key ECD interventions would tend to be higher in the districts located in the better-off provinces.

The chapter provides the results of the application of the SABER-ECD diagnostic tool to the five districts (see chapter 2 for the application of the tool at the national level). The structure of the chapter is as follows. Given that the SABER-ECD framework has already been presented in chapter 2, each of the next three chapters is devoted to a policy goal. A conclusion follows.

Establishing an Enabling Environment

As shown in table 4.2, the five districts are rated at the same level (emerging) in terms of their policies related to establishing an enabling environment. District ratings are slightly less than those observed for Indonesia as a whole, but differences are small as shown in figure 4.1. In that figure, as well as in many others that follow, the districts are ranked on the horizontal axis according to the level of GDP per capita of the province in which they are located. There is a presumption that for some of the indicators—including those related to finance and the coverage of various programs—richer areas tend to perform better than poorer areas. When considering policy frameworks, this is not necessarily the case, but when considering which interventions actually reach the target population, richer areas typically do perform better. Note also that while normalized ratings are provided in tables (taking a value of one to four), the actual ratings obtained

Table 4.2 Enabling Environment Policy Goal and Levers

	Policy goal	Levers		
	Enabling environment	Legal framework	Intesectoral coordination	Finance
Indonesia district				
Kapuas	2	2	1	3
Manggarai Timur	2	2	1	3
Pacitan	2	2	2	3
Sukabumi	2	2	3	2
Sumbawa	2	2	3	2
All five districts	2	2	2	2.6
Countries				
Indonesia	3	3	3	3
All countries	2.1	2.4	1.9	2.1

Note: Each number indicates the level of development in early childhood development policy at the corresponding level. "1"= latent, "2"= emerging, "3"= established, and "4" = advanced.

Figure 4.1 Ratings for Enabling Environment Policy Goals

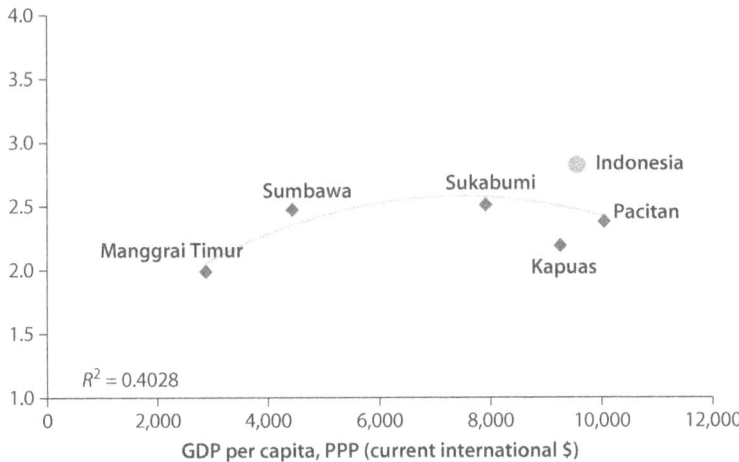

Note: GDP = gross domestic product; PPP = purchasing power parity.

from responses to a range of questions are displayed in the figures, so that even when two districts have the same normalized rating, there can still be differences in actual ratings.

In the case of the enabling environment policy goal, differences between districts tend to be small. This should not be too surprising, given that many of the policies related to the enabling environment—such as the legal framework—tend to be decided at the national level, and this may actually result in some cases in lower ratings at the district than at the national level. But there are nevertheless some differences between districts in ratings. In what follows, we discuss the findings for the various districts for each of the three policy levers.

Legal Framework

Consider first the legal framework, where, as shown in figure 4.2, differences between districts are small. This can be illustrated in the case of health services. By the time the data collection was held in five districts, the former insurance scheme for maternal health (*Jaminan Persalinan, Jampersal*) was still implemented. In all five districts, because of national-level policies, the government-funded maternal and baby health insurance scheme (*Jampersal*) covers the costs of antenatal care, childbirth and skilled delivery, postnatal care, and family planning services for all mothers and their babies. Young children receive a course of immunizations, and well-child visits are required at post natal periods, at least four times until 42 days after childbirth and periodic visits until five years of age. These well-child visits are provided free of charge at village health posts (*Posyandu*). Currently, the former insurance scheme has been replaced by the national health insurance scheme (*Jaminan Kesehatan Nasional*, JKN) covering promotion, preventive, curative, and rehabilitative health services. While the health sector generally provides a good range of basic services, the system could be further strengthened to improve the provision of health services: required immunizations could be expanded to include vaccination for rubella, meningitis, and mumps; and quality health screenings for human immunodeficiency virus (HIV) and sexually transmitted diseases should available at all heath centers.

Figure 4.2 Ratings for Legal Framework Policy Levers

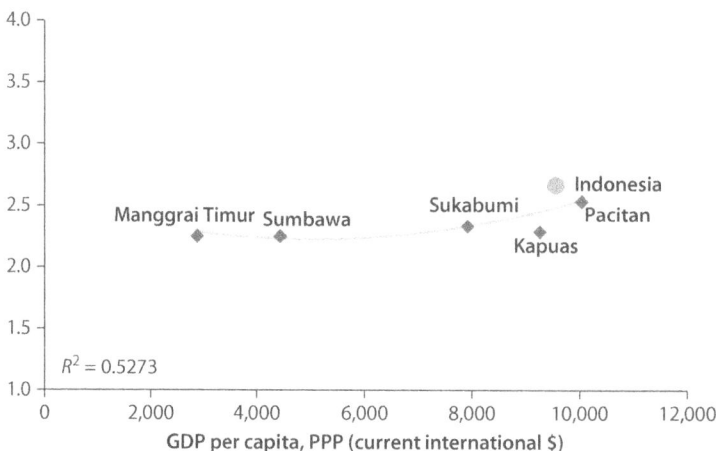

Note: GDP = gross domestic product; PPP = purchasing power parity.

While policies are relatively good in health, free preprimary education is not mandated, neither nationally nor in the five districts. While it may not be realistic at this point to require children to attend preprimary school free of charge, districts could consider this as a goal to work towards. Attending high-quality preprimary programs helps prepare children for future academic and social success and, more broadly, strengthens the economy and society. In the near term, expanding access to programs that teach parents how to promote their children's development can be an effective way to foster learning at home, especially in poorer families.

Again, at the district level, there is in most cases no policy to mandate birth registration, as all districts defer to national policy on birth registration. The exception is Manggarai Timur, which mandates that all newborns be registered through the Office of Civil Registration within 60 days after delivery (District Regulation No. 1/2012 on Civil Registration).

Finally, and this is again observed in all five districts (as well as nationally), while some child and social protection services are established, these could be improved. But there have also been initiatives at the district level. For example, several districts have established integrated service centers for women and children to prevent domestic violence. In addition, district social affairs offices focus on advocacy and treatment of women and children affected by trauma. While this type of initiative is commendable, there is still room for improvement to strengthen social protection policies and services not only in Kapuas, but also in other districts.

Districts typically do not have policies to provide orphans and vulnerable children with ECD services. Furthermore, there are typically no laws or statutes in place to protect the rights of children with disabilities and promote their participation and access to ECD services. However, in Pacitan the local government has established an inclusive education policy (District Regulation No. 38/2012 on Inclusive Education) to cater to the needs of young children with disabilities. The regulation defines children with special needs as children with different physical and/or mental disability, requiring special interventions for disorders such as sight, hearing, communication, physical, mental, socioemotional, and autism. The local government ensures that at least one early childhood care and education (ECCE) facility and one elementary school in every subdistrict are supported by teachers with special skills and have proper educative toys accessible to young children.

Intersectoral Coordination

Consider next intersectoral coordination (Fiugre 4.3) where there are more differences in the ratings for the five districts than was the case for the legal framework, as shown in figure 4.2. Sukabumi and Sumbawa are rated as established in terms of their intersectoral coordination mechanisms, Pacitan is rated as emerging, and Kapuas and Manggarai Timur are rated as latent.

A key reason while the Kapuas and Manggarai Timur districts are rated as latent is that they do not appear to have an explicitly stated multisectoral ECD policy that would complement the national Holistic Integrated-Early Childhood

Figure 4.3 Ratings for Intersectoral Coordination Policy Lever

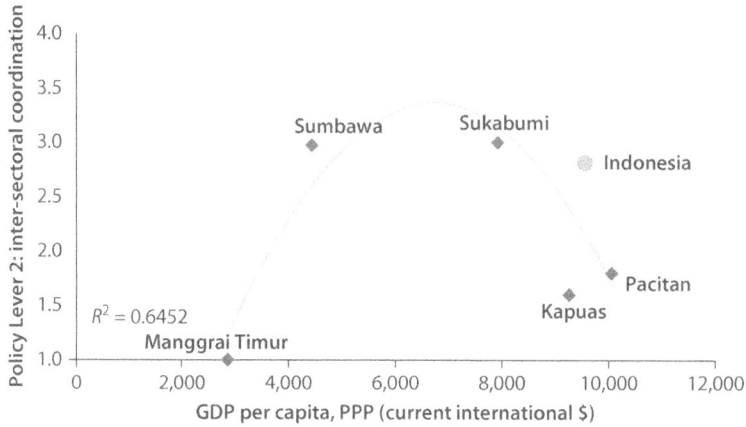

Note: GDP = gross domestic product; PPP = purchasing power parity.

Development (HI-ECD) policy. The two districts also have not established a district cross-sectoral ECD institutional anchor, even though the Manggarai Timur district is planning to initiate a pilot early childhood care and education (ECCE) project targeting children from birth to age six years that would provide holistic ECD services including early stimulation, health, nutrition, and parenting services. This project will be implemented through multisectoral agreement between the relevant sectors, as well as integrated budget framework. Lessons learned from this initiative could serve as a basis for the development of a holistic and integrated ECD system in Manggarai Timur, including all relevant sectors (education, health, nutrition, and child and social protection) and targeting the most vulnerable children.

By contrast, Sumbawa has an explicitly stated multisectoral ECD strategy. The Regent's Decree on Holistic and Integrated ECD (*Pospa BKB* [HI-ECD]) policy was established in 2013 for children 0–72 months. The HI-ECD policy includes an implementation plan, and funding comes from local budget and community participation. The policy covers education, health, nutrition, and child protection. The HI-ECD could be reviewed to ensure that it covers social protection, which protects the most vulnerable children and their families. In addition, an institutional anchor has been established to coordinate ECD across sectors. The district planning and development agency (Badan Perencanaan dan Pembangunan Daerah, *Bappeda*) is the lead coordination body for ECD policy. In 2013, *Bappeda* formed the Taskforce of HI-ECD (*Pospa BKB*) as the cross-sectoral district ECD anchor. Members of the taskforce, including the district education office, district health office, district social affairs, family planning and women empowerment agency, district community empowerment and village governance, and the district religious affairs office are responsible for implementation. The *Pospa BKP* provides general guidance on a list of integrated ECD services for young children, and detailed manuals for service delivery are provided by each of the leading sectors responsible for implementation of ECD services.

Similarly, Sukabumi has a HI-ECD policy that is multisectoral and encompasses education, health, nutrition, and child protection. The policy does not yet cover social protection, a sector that includes issues such as services for orphans and vulnerable children and financial transfers or income supports for vulnerable families. It could be reviewed to ensure it aids the district's most vulnerable children. The *Bappeda* (district planning and development agency) is the lead coordination body for ECD policy. Implementation is conducted by the district education office, district health office, district social affairs, family planning and women empowerment agency, district community empowerment and village governance, district religious affairs office, ECCE teacher associations, and civil society organizations. The ECD Forum and Women Group and other meetings between service providers and local government help to coordinate service delivery. It is not fully clear whether the *Bappeda* has the resources and authority to fulfill its mandate as the ECD leader and coordination body.

Pacitan has a rating of emerging for intersectoral coordination. While a multisectoral ECD strategy has not yet been developed at the district level, the district follows the provincial strategy. The government is also implementing the HI-ECD (*Taman Posyandu*) based on East Java Provincial Government's Regulation No. 63/2011 on HI-ECD. Since decentralization, the district government has developed complementary ECD policies and programs funded through local budgets. While the education sector leads the ECD policy development, the *Bappeda* (district planning and development agency) leads coordination efforts at the implementation level. The multisectors stakeholders involved include district education office, district health office, district social affairs office, family planning and women empowerment agency (*BP2KB*), district community empowerment and village governance office (*Bappemas*), district religious affairs office, ECD partners, and ECCE teachers associations.

Apart from the issues of ECD district strategies and coordination bodies, it is important to note that in most districts ECD implementers tend to coordinate services at the level of delivery. In Sumbawa, for example, the teachers associations include the *IGTK* (for kindergarten teachers), *IGRA* (for Islamic kindergarten teachers), and *HIMPAUDI* (for nonformal ECCE teachers). Cross-association meetings between teachers and other ECD partners, such as the ECD Forum and Women's Group, take place every three months at the district level (the same types of teacher associations exist in Pacitan, also with quarterly meetings). The district education office and district religious affairs office direct the ECCE sector, which encompasses formal programs (mainly kindergartens and Islamic kindergartens) and nonformal programs (daycare centers and playgroups). The Ministry of Religious Affairs sets policy and budgets for Islamic kindergartens; the district religious affairs office conducts monitoring of the schools. The Ministry of Education and Culture and district education office are responsible for kindergartens, playgroups, daycare, and other types of ECCE services. In Kapuas as well, ECD implementers coordinate at the level of service delivery. ECCE teachers have regular monthly meetings held by the ECCE teacher association (Himpaudi or IGTKI). In addition, coordination meetings are held quarterly for all ECCE service providers, Women Group, and ECCE Supervisor Association.

In Manggarai Timur, the education sector leads the ECD policy development, and every village is required to at least have one type of ECCE service that covers children from birth to age six years. In health and nutrition sectors, the focus is on children younger than five years of age, and parenting education services target parents with children from birth to age six years. Program implementers do not appear to meet regularly at the subdistrict or village level. Unlike the other districts studied, teacher associations do not seem to coordinate meetings for ECD implementers.

Finance

There are some differences between districts in the ratings for the finance policy lever, but these tend not to be very large as shown in figure 4.4. Still, while three districts are rated as established (Kapuas, Manggarai Timur, and Pacitan), the other two are rated as emerging (Sukabumi and Sumbawa), in part because of differences in the use of funding criteria.

The ECD budget process in Kapuas appears to be transparent. Explicit criteria are used to decide ECD spending in the education, health, nutrition sectors, and the district government can accurately report ECD expenditures. The family planning and women empowerment agency and district social affairs office report expenditures for all beneficiaries, but do not report expenditures specifically for ECD-aged children. The district planning and development agency, education office, health office, social affairs office, family planning and women

Figure 4.4 Ratings for Finance Policy Levers

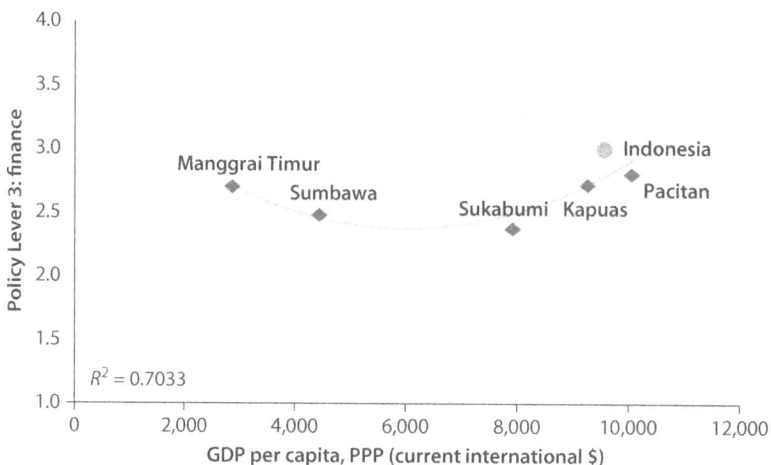

Note: GDP = gross domestic product; PPP = purchasing power parity.

empowerment agency, and community empowerment and village governance office coordinate through joint planning sessions to share budgets. Budget planning documents are submitted to local parliament for assessment and approvals. In 2013, 37 percent of total government expenditures went towards public education, but only 0.2 percent of public education funding is spent on ECCE. The district government makes monthly payments to ECCE staff at public and private facilities. In spite of this, the minimum compensation for ECCE teachers is only one-third of the minimum primary school teacher compensation. The pay scale for kindergarten teachers is higher than that of nonformal ECCE teachers. Overall, because public support for ECCE is limited, parents may be required to pay for tuition, uniform, meals, and materials.

In Manggarai Timur as well, the local government uses explicit criteria to determine funding allocations for ECD in the health and nutrition sectors, giving consideration to number of children covered, children's characteristics such as gender, socioeconomic status, special needs, as well as geographical location for nutrition funding solely. For other sectors, explicit formulas tend not to be used. Sectoral ministries coordinate to determine their budgets for ECD and budget planning documents are submitted to local parliament for assessment and approvals. The local government can report public ECD expenditures across health, nutrition, and education sectors. In 2013, 38.6 percent of the total government expenditures went towards public education, but as in Kapuas only 0.4 percent of public education funding is spent on ECCE. The family planning and women empowerment agency reports expenditures used to fund activities related to institutional strengthening, gender mainstreaming, and socialization of women and child protection activities but not specific to ECD-aged children. Similarly, the district social affairs office reports expenditures for all beneficiaries used for activities such as socialization and assistance. The local government makes monthly payments to ECCE staff in government and nongovernment facilities. Kindergarten teachers are compensated with the same minimum salary as primary school teachers. In addition, teachers in community-based centers such as toddler-family group, daycare, and other ECCE services receive incentives from the local government, but because of limited budget only teachers from a few centers received the incentive.

In Pacitan, Sumbawa, and Sukabumi, with the exception of early childhood nutrition funding, the local governments do not use explicit criteria or formulas to determine how funds for ECD services are allocated across sectors. For nutrition funding, consideration is given to number of children covered, location, and historical precedent. As in other districts, sectoral ministries coordinate to determine budgets for ECD, and budget planning documents are submitted to local parliament for assessment and approvals. Public ECD expenditures in most categories are reported in these three districts. In 2013, only 5 percent of total government expenditures in Pacitan went towards public education, a much lower proportion than elsewhere; for Sumbawa and Sukabumi the proportion is much higher (34 percent for Sumbawa). But in the three districts as in other districts, less than 1 percent of public education funding is spent on ECCE. ECCE staffs in government and nongovernment facilities receive monthly compensation from the local government. In Pacitan, kindergarten teachers are compensated with the same minimum salary as primary school teachers, with salaries depending on the grade level at appointment, and teachers in community-based ECCE centers and other ECCE services receive incentives from the local government. By contrast in Sumbawa, the minimum ECCE teacher compensation is only 10 percent of the minimum primary school teacher compensation. In many cases, parents have to contribute fees to ECCE centers, with fees potentially include tuition, desk fees, and fees for parent–teacher associations. In Sukabumi as well, ECCE teachers are compensated at far lower levels than primary school teachers. This difference in pay for ECCE teachers explains why Sumbawa and Sukabumi contribute to lower ratings for the policy lever.

Implementing Widely Policy Goal and Levers

As shown in table 4.3 and as depicted in figure 4.5, Pacitan is rated at a higher level than the other four districts in terms of policies and programs related to implementing widely. This is in part because the coverage of programs is higher in Pacitan, which is not too surprising since among the five districts Pacitan is located in the richest province. The assessment of equity in ECD programs and policies tends to yield the lowest ratings of the three policy levers in part because of large differences between groups and areas in program coverage, but it must be noted that this is due in part to imputations of national level data, given the lack of detailed data by group or areas within districts. In what follows, we discuss the findings for each of the three policy levers.

Table 4.3 Implementing Widely Policy Goal and Levers

	Policy goal	Levers		
	Implementing widely	Scope of programs	Coverage of programs	Equity
Indonesia district				
Kapuas	2	2	2	2
Manggarai Timur	2	2	2	1
Pacitan	3	3	3	2
Sukabumi	2	3	2	2
Sumbawa	2	3	2	1
All five districts	2.2	2.6	2.2	1.6
Countries				
Indonesia	2	3	2	2
All countries	2.4	2.5	2.6	2.3

Note: Each number indicates the level of development in early childhood development policy at the national level. "1"= latent, "2"= emerging, "3"= established, and "4" = advanced.

Figure 4.5 Ratings in Implementing Widely Policy Goal

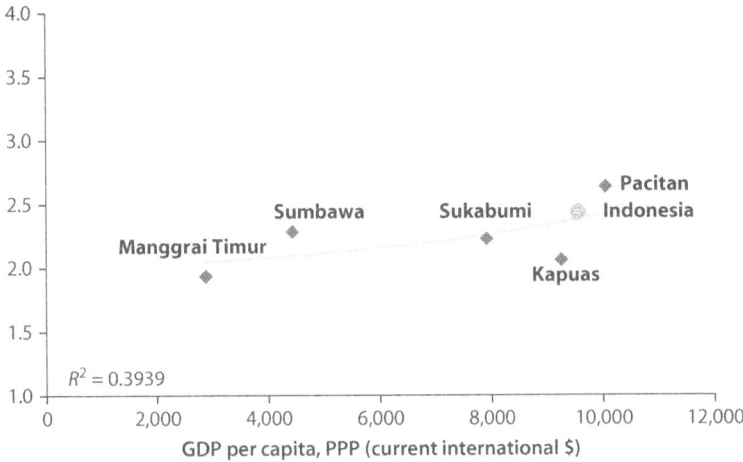

Note: GDP = gross domestic product; PPP = purchasing power parity.

Scope of Programs

The ratings for the scope of programs are slightly lower in Kapuas and Manggarai Timur than they are in Pacitan, Sukabumi, and Sumbawa, but overall quite a few programs are available in all five districts, at least in principle, even though there are differences between sectors. As an illustration, figure 4.6 displays the scope of programs available in Pacitan by sector and beneficiary group—this corresponding visualization is fairly similar for the other districts.

Programs are established in Pacitan (and the other districts) across all relevant sectors and beneficiary groups (see figure 4.7). Although the Pacitan district government has not yet issued policy related to HI-ECD (*Taman Posyandu*), programs are being implemented in line with the East Java Provincial Regulation No. 63/2011on HI-ECD. The District Health Office provides a wide range of health and nutrition interventions for pregnant women and their young children. Through *Taman Posyandu*, integrated ECD services are delivered by village health post, toddler family group or BKB, and ECCE. The District Education and Religious offices provide early learning opportunities for young children. In line with the regulation on inclusive education, the education office ensures the existence of one inclusive ECCE facility in every subdistrict at minimum. The District Social Office has established the Family Hope program, which provides conditional cash transfers to low-income families for accessing ECD services. The office also provides counselling services for children facing social problems. The District Civil Registration Office implements SILADES, a program through which communities in remote areas/villages directly register their newborns without going to district capital city. While it is commendable that a wide range of programs are available in Pacitan and the other districts, the scale of service delivery is also an important consideration, and as will be discussed in the

Figure 4.6 Scope of Programs in Pacitan District

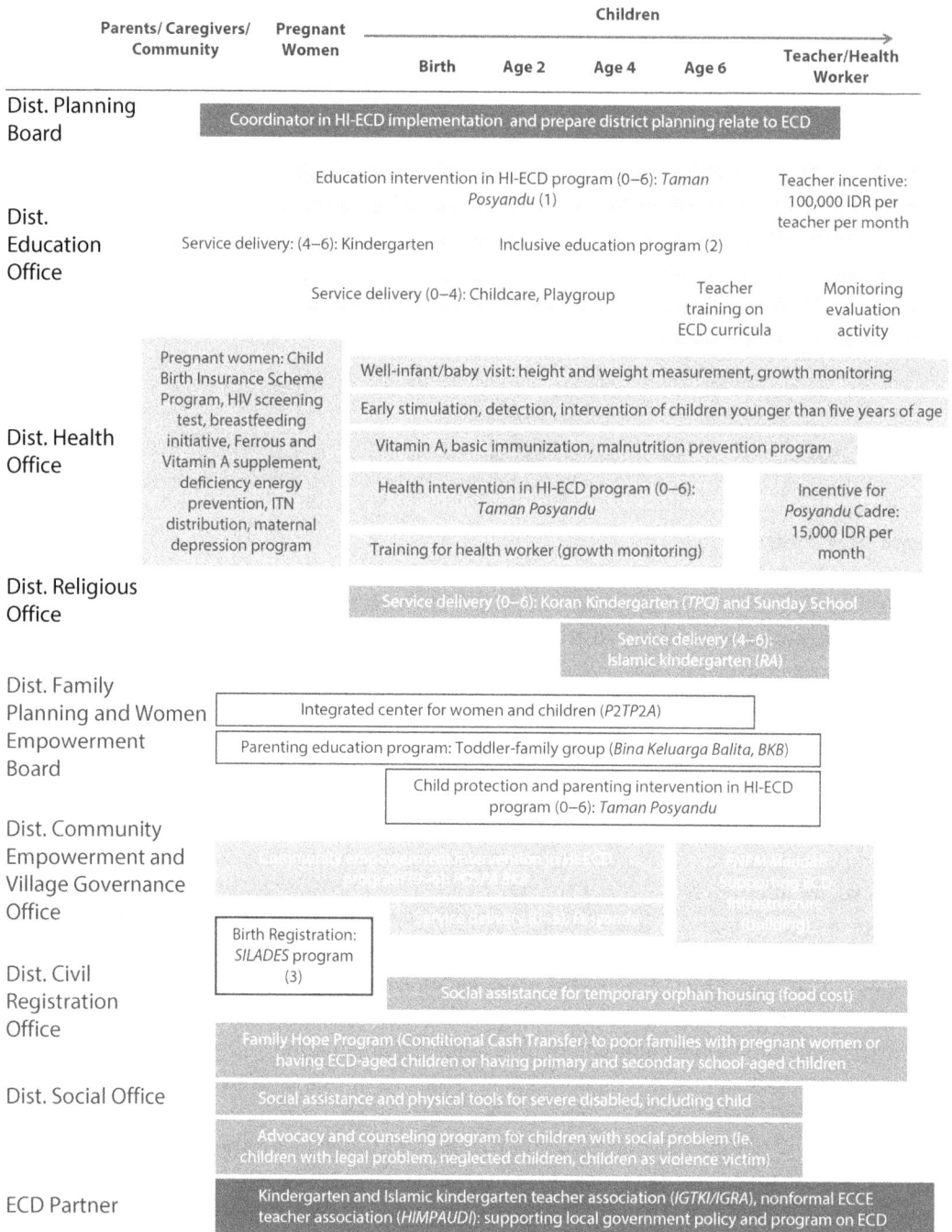

	Parents/ Caregivers/ Community	Pregnant Women	Children				
			Birth	Age 2	Age 4	Age 6	Teacher/Health Worker

Dist. Planning Board
Coordinator in HI-ECD implementation and prepare district planning relate to ECD

Dist. Education Office
Education intervention in HI-ECD program (0–6): *Taman Posyandu* (1)
Teacher incentive: 100,000 IDR per teacher per month
Service delivery: (4–6): Kindergarten
Inclusive education program (2)
Service delivery (0–4): Childcare, Playgroup
Teacher training on ECD curricula
Monitoring evaluation activity

Dist. Health Office
Pregnant women: Child Birth Insurance Scheme Program, HIV screening test, breastfeeding initiative, Ferrous and Vitamin A supplement, deficiency energy prevention, ITN distribution, maternal depression program
Well-infant/baby visit: height and weight measurement, growth monitoring
Early stimulation, detection, intervention of children younger than five years of age
Vitamin A, basic immunization, malnutrition prevention program
Health intervention in HI-ECD program (0–6): *Taman Posyandu*
Training for health worker (growth monitoring)
Incentive for *Posyandu* Cadre: 15,000 IDR per month

Dist. Religious Office
Service delivery (0–6): Koran Kindergarten (*TPQ*) and Sunday School
Service delivery (4–6): Islamic kindergarten (*RA*)

Dist. Family Planning and Women Empowerment Board
Integrated center for women and children (*P2TP2A*)
Parenting education program: Toddler-family group (*Bina Keluarga Balita, BKB*)
Child protection and parenting intervention in HI-ECD program (0–6): *Taman Posyandu*

Dist. Community Empowerment and Village Governance Office
Community empowerment intervention in HI-ECD program (0–6): *POSYANDU*
PNPM Mandiri: supporting ECD infrastructure (building)
Service delivery (0–5): *Posyandu*

Dist. Civil Registration Office
Birth Registration: *SILADES* program (3)
Social assistance for temporary orphan housing (food cost)

Dist. Social Office
Family Hope Program (Conditional Cash Transfer) to poor families with pregnant women or having ECD-aged children or having primary and secondary school-aged children
Social assistance and physical tools for severe disabled, including child
Advocacy and counseling program for children with social problem (ie. children with legal problem, neglected children, children as violence victim)

ECD Partner
Kindergarten and Islamic kindergarten teacher association (*IGTKI/IGRA*), nonformal ECCE teacher association (*HIMPAUDI*): supporting local government policy and program on ECD

Note: ECCE = early childhood care and education; ECD = early childhood development; IDR = Indonesian rupiah; PNPM = *Program Nasional Pemberdayaan Masyarakat* (National Program for Community Empowerment).

Figure 4.7 Ratings for Scope of Program Policy Lever

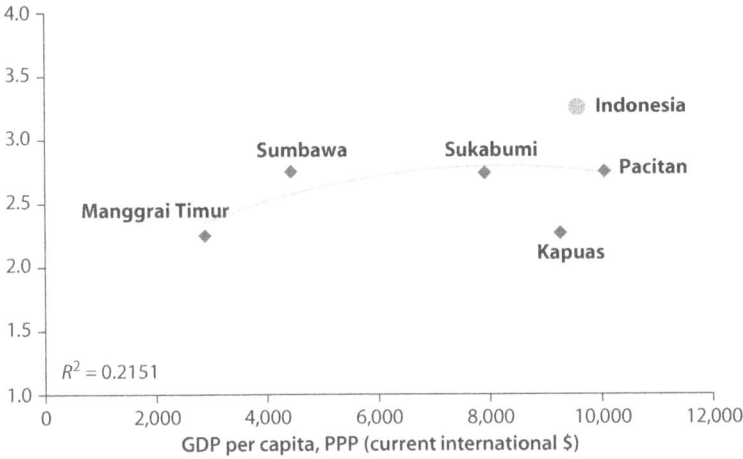

Note: GDP = gross domestic product; PPP = purchasing power parity.

next chapter, coverage is at times low. In addition, programs tend to be more limited in scope in the areas of child and social protection. Antipoverty interventions and programs targeted towards orphans and vulnerable children or children with special needs do not exist, for example.

Coverage of Programs

As shown in table 4.3 and figure 4.8, the ratings for the coverage of programs are the same for all districts except Pacitan which has a higher rating (established as opposed to emerging). This is not surprising since among the five districts Pacitan is located in the richest province. Information on coverage for a few specific ECD interventions is provided in table 4.4.

In Kapuas, Pacitan, and Sumbawa, the coverage of antenatal care and skilled delivery are greater than 90 percent, while in Manggarai Timur and Sukabumi, coverage rates are lower. In four of the five districts, immunization against diphtheria, pertussis, and tetanus (DPT) is near universal, but the rate is lower in Sukabumi. By contrast, the share of children younger than five years of age with suspected pneumonia who receive antibiotics is much lower, with the highest rate observed for Pacitan at 47.6 percent. Pacitan also has the highest coverage rates for vitamin A supplementation for children 6–59 months (at 93.5 percent), with Manggarai Timur having the lowest rate at 57.3 percent. In Kapuas, only a very small minority of children are exclusively breastfed, with the rates being less than half for Sukabami and higher for the other two districts. Gross enrollment in preprimary education is below one-third, except for Pacitan where it is at 60.3 percent—in general as many girls attend preschools as boys. The birth registration rate in Kapuas at 43.9 percent is much higher than in Manggarai Timur, but much lower than in Pacitan where special programs have been put in place. (Data were not available for the other districts.)

Figure 4.8 Ratings for Coverage of Programs Policy Lever

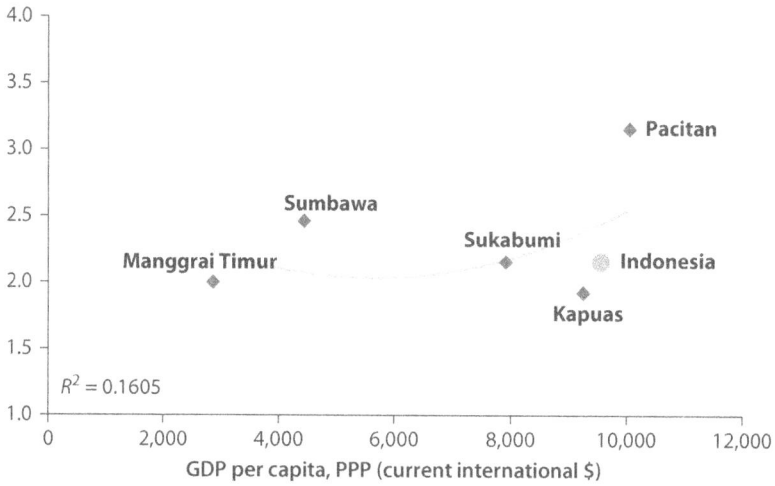

Note: GDP = gross domestic product; PPP = purchasing power parity.

Table 4.4 Coverage of Selected Early Childhood Development Programs by District

	Kapuas	Manggarai Timur	Pacitan	Sukabumi	Sumbawa
Births attended by a skilled attendant	91.5	77.0	96.5	82.6	95.1
Pregnant women who attend at least four antenatal visits	90.7	83.0	91.9	83.9	92.8
One-year-old children immunized against DPT3	97.7	119.0[a]	102.4[a]	91.6	100.0
Children with suspected pneumonia getting antibiotics	0.8	22.8	47.6	36.2	—
Vitamin A supplementation, children 6–59 months	74.3	57.3	93.5	87.1	92.7
Exclusive breastfeeding until 6 months	4.0	78.1	82.1	41.0	76.3
Gross preprimary enrollment rate	23.6	24.0	60.3	23.7	31.8
Preprimary enrollment ratio of boys to girls	1.03	0.94	1.03	0.96	1.01
Birth registration rate	43.9	2.0	87.8	—	—

Source: Health Office of Kapuas District (2013); Health Office of Manggarai Timur District (2013); Health, Education, and Population Registration Office of Pacitan District (2012), Health Office of District (2013), and Health Office of Sumbawa District (2013).
Note: DPT = diphtheria, pertussis, and tetanus. — = not available.
a. In Manggarai Timur district, 5,451 children younger than one year old received DPT3 immunization out of 4,559 children targeted (119 percent). Similarly in Pacitan district, 7,700 children younger than one year old received DPT3 immunization out of 7,518 children targeted (102.4 percent). These high rates of DPT3 immunization coverage in these two districts may be attributed to the inclusion of immunized children who resided in the neighborhood districts.

Equity

The ratings for equity are slightly higher in Kapuas, Pacitan, and Sukabumi, than in Manggarai Timur and Sumbawa, but overall all districts are rated low, at the latent or emerging level (see figure 4.9). This is in part because data are often not available at the district level on equity in the coverage of programs. For that reason, values at the national level were imputed, and since there is a lot of inequality in coverage at the national level between quintiles or by geographic area, this translates through in the imputation at the district level. But apart from differences in coverage rates between groups, additional information is used to assign ratings, including for the availability of instruction in local languages, and the existence of policies for vuln,erable groups, for example to serve children with special needs or orphans and vulnerable children.

In Kapuas, the curriculum and teacher materials are not translated to promote mother tongue instruction. While mother tongue instruction is not mandated in Manggarai Timur, the local government encourages it, and at times the local language is used in order to make instructional materials easier to be understood. Yet, *Bahasa* Indonesian remains as the standard language. Pacitan has an inclusive education policy which guarantees the provision of ECCE services to children with special needs, and while mother tongue instruction is not mandated, it is encouraged and sometimes the local language is used in order to make the instructional materials more easily understood. In Sukabami, no mechanisms appear to currently exist to ensure access to services for children with special needs. Mother tongue instruction is not mandated but is sometimes used in preprimary education to facilitate learning. Finally, Sumbawa also does not have an inclusive education policy and does not guarantee ECCE services to children with special needs. Mother tongue instruction is again encouraged but not mandated.

Figure 4.9 Ratings for Equity Policy Lever

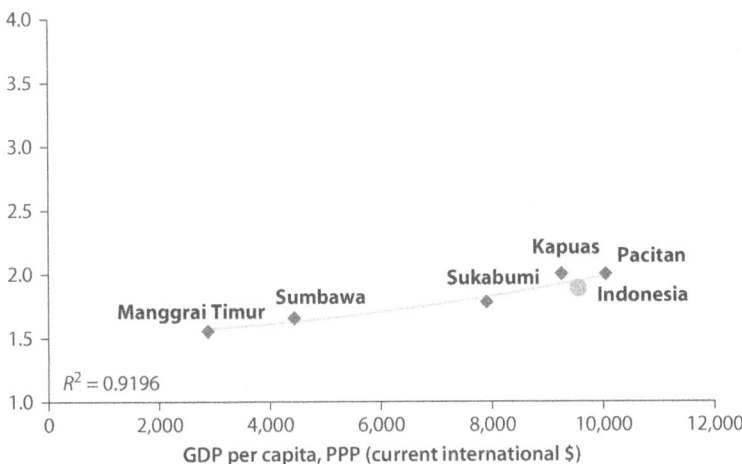

Note: GDP = gross domestic product; PPP = purchasing power parity.

Monitoring and Assuring Quality Policy Goal and Levers

As shown in table 4.5, with the exception of Kapuas that is rated as emerging, all districts are rated as established for the monitoring and quality policy goal. Ratings for data availability are the same (emerging) for all districts (See Figure 4.10), and the same is observed for quality standards, although there the ratings are higher (established). There are more differences between districts for the compliance with standards. In what follows, findings for each of the policy levers are provided.

Table 4.5   Benchmarking the Monitoring and Quality Policy Goals

	Policy goal	Levers		
	Monitoring and quality	Data availability	Quality standards	Compliance with standards
Indonesia district				
Kapuas	2	2	3	2
Manggarai Timur	3	2	3	2
Pacitan	3	2	3	3
Sukabumi	3	2	3	2
Sumbawa	3	2	3	3
All five districts	2.8	2	3	2.4
Countries				
Indonesia	2.5	3	2.9	1.7
All countries	2.1	2.1	2.5	1.6

Note: Each number indicates the level of development in early childhood development policy at the national level. "1"= latent, "2"= emerging, "3"= established, and "4"= advanced.

Figure 4.10   Ratings for Monitoring and Assuring Quality Policy Goal

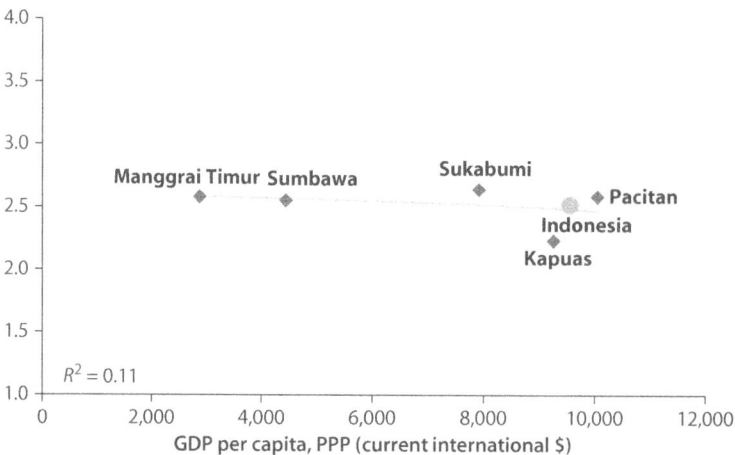

Note: GDP = gross domestic product; PPP = purchasing power parity.

Data Availability

All five districts have the same rating in terms of data availability. This is because in all five districts, limited administrative data are available on ECD programs and outcomes (see figure 4.11). Data are collected on young children's enrollment in preschools and usage of health, nutrition, and some protection services. Data on children's access to some ECD services by gender are also collected, but typically information is not available within districts by socioeconomic status, location, ethnicity, mother tongue, or special needs status. The national household surveys are representative at the provincial level only and therefore cannot be used for district-level assessments. Inequalities in child development begin in the prenatal period and increase over time without necessary interventions. Good data are needed to implement correcting measures.

Indicators to measure physical, cognitive, language, and social development are also typically not collected. Tracking individual outcomes can indicate when extra services are necessary for children with developmental difficulties. One example of a comprehensive tracking system is found in Chile, under its new ECD policy, Chile *Crece Contigo*. The policy includes a bio-psychosocial development support program that tracks the development path of all children who are covered by the public health system (75 percent of Chile's children). The health sector plays a central role, providing most of the services and screening, but the intervention allows for differentiated support to the most vulnerable children, tracking their development comprehensively and intervening with multisectoral services when necessary.

Figure 4.11 Ratings for Data Availability Policy Lever

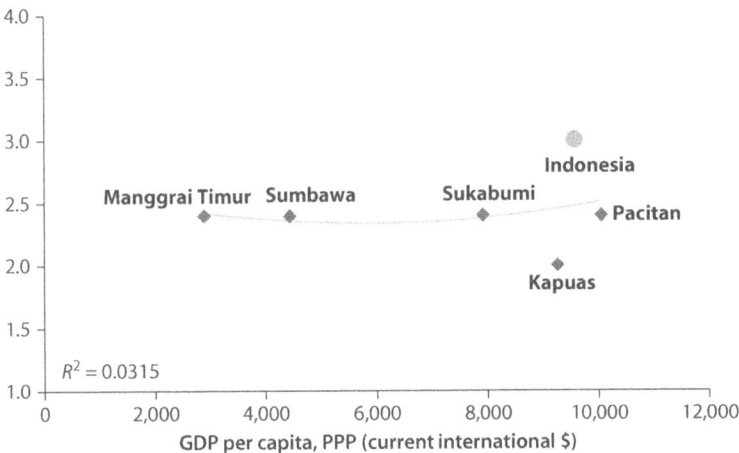

Note: GDP = gross domestic product; PPP = purchasing power parity.

Quality Standards

As for data availability, all five districts have the same rating for quality standards (see figure 4.12). Learning standards for ECCE have been established nationally. In 2009, the Directorate General of the Ministry of Education and Culture established the early childhood education and development (ECED) Learning Standard through Ministerial Regulation no. 58/2009. The teacher-to-child ratio standards are as 1:6 for birth to two-year-olds; 1:10 for two- to five-year-olds; and 1:15 for five- to six-year-olds. The standards also include motor, cognitive, language, socioemotional, art, and religious/morality areas for children ages 0–72 months. The standards are evidence based and stem from ECED studies in Indonesia. However, mechanisms are not in place to enforce the standards, as will be discussed in the next chapter. In addition, there is no clear effort to ensure coherence and continuum between the preprimary and primary curricula. School supervisors are responsible for monitoring and evaluation of the learning process and for maintaining quality, but these activities are not formally regulated. As part of a World Bank project, the Directorate of Teachers and Educators in the Ministry is developing monitoring and evaluation tools and a manual for ECCE school supervisors. The manual and tools are expected to be formally adopted by the central government to help supervise ECCE centers.

The ministry has set infrastructure and construction requirements for ECCE facilities, including standards for functional hygienic facilities and potable water sources. However, no specific policy exists to inspect the quality of ECCE centers for construction and infrastructure, and registration and accreditation procedures are not in place for ECCE facilities. The policy on construction standards is currently being reviewed and is expected to cover all ECCE facilities.

Standards for preservice qualifications are established for ECCE service providers, again at the national level. The Ministry of Education and Culture has

Figure 4.12 Ratings for Quality Standards Policy Lever

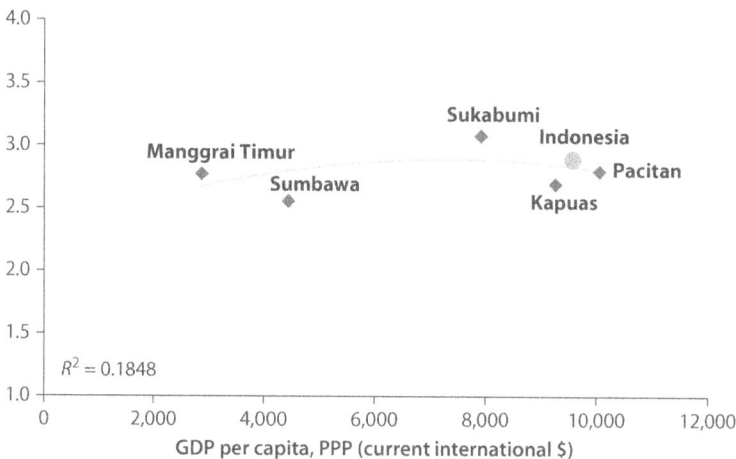

Note: GDP = gross domestic product; PPP = purchasing power parity.

established qualification standards for caregivers and ECCE teachers under Ministerial Regulation No. 16/2007. ECCE teachers *(guru)* for five- and six-year-olds are required to have a specialized tertiary degree in ECD or psychology. ECCE teacher assistants *(guru pendamping)* are required to have a diploma degree in kindergarten schooling or upper-secondary school completion with certified ECCE training. Caregivers *(pengasuh)* are required to have completed secondary school. The district education offices manage preservice and in-service teacher training. In-service training is mandatory and is regulated through ECCE teacher training manual by the directorate general of early childhood education. It consists of a tiered training program comprising 48 hours basic training, 64 hours medium learning, 80 hours advanced learning, and a fieldwork practicum. ECCE teachers are required to take a preservice fieldwork practicum. Thus, a total of about 200 hour preservice practicum *(Tugas Mandiri)* is mandated for ECCE teachers. Standards are also in place for health workers. For example, village midwives and officers from district health offices are required to complete training in ECD, and as is the case for ECCE centers, there are construction standards established for health centers and hospitals.

Compliance with Standards

Mechanisms to track compliance with standards for ECCE services could be improved in all five districts, although Pacitan and Sumbawa are doing slightly better according to the ratings (see figure 4.13). As mentioned in the previous chapter, no policy for inspection of ECCE centers exists and compliance with construction standards is not monitored. Centers tend to comply with service delivery standards. For example, in Kapuas the average teacher-to-child ratio is 1:8, which is conducive to a strong learning environment. Some centers are

Figure 4.13 Ratings for Compliance with Standards Policy Lever

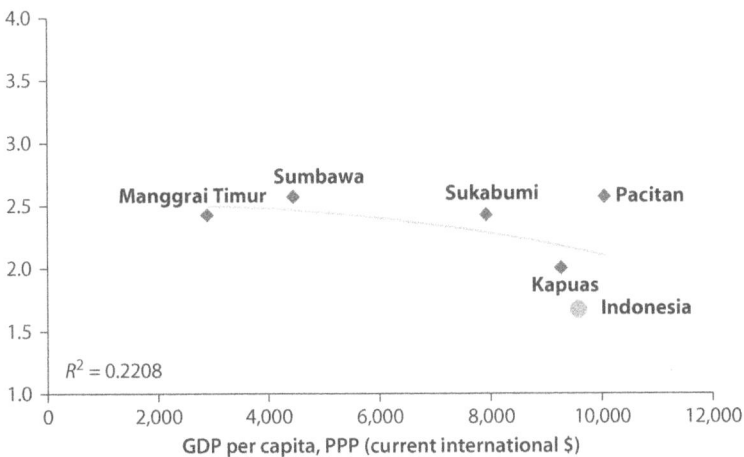

GDP per capita, PPP (current international $)

$R^2 = 0.2208$

Note: GDP = gross domestic product; PPP = purchasing power parity.

Early Childhood Education and Development in Indonesia • http://dx.doi.org/10.1596/978-1-4648-0646-9

opened only for a few hours per week, well below the international best practice standard of at least 15 hours per week.

There are some differences between districts in terms of compliance with regulation on the level of education required for ECCE teachers. In Kapuas, 974 of the 994 ECCE teachers have the required level of education. In Pacitan, among 2,510 ECCE professionals, 87 percent have completed upper-secondary school, a proportion slightly higher than in Sukabami (83 percent). In Sumbawa, the proportion is even higher at 92 percent (2,445 of 2,667 ECCE teachers). In Manggarai Timur, the proportion is however lower, with 98 of 180 nonformal ECCE teachers having the required level of schooling, but those who do not have the necessary formal qualifications receive in-service training from the district education office. Teachers without the required level of education receive in-service training from district education offices.

In general, when policies exist, the desired outcomes can be quite good, including in terms of program coverage. But the lack of policies on some important issues often correlates with poor outcomes, and simply having a policy may not be enough. This highlights the need to put in place regulatory and monitoring frameworks for all key ECD interventions.

Conclusion

In the context of substantial decentralization for ECD policies and programs in Indonesia, this chapter has provided results from the implementation of SABER-ECD tool in five illustrative districts. While on some dimensions the performance of the districts is similar, in other dimensions there are differences. Table 4.6 provides the ratings obtained by each of the five districts for the nine policy levers. On average, across all policy levers, Pacitan, the district located in the richest province, has the highest ratings (average rating of 2.6). Manggarai Timur, the district located in the poorest province, has the lowest ratings (average rating of 2.0). However, for the other three districts, the average ratings do not follow the level of economic development of the provinces in which the districts are located. Of these three districts, Kapuas has the lowest average rating (value of 2.1), while it is in the richest of the three provinces. The average rating for Sukabumi and Sumbawa is 2.3. With the notable exception of Kapuas, which seems to be underperforming, the ranking based on the average ratings for SABER-ECD policy levers is the same as the ranking based on the level of economic development of their province. Still, the association between both variables appears limited.

What are some of the broad policy recommendations that could be made on the basis of these results? Specific recommendations would typically require additional analysis. In terms of the enabling environment, given that districts are responsible for the implementation of ECD policies and programs, it would make sense for the districts that have not yet done so to adopt district-level multisectoral ECD strategies and to define a menu of essential services to be

Table 4.6 Comparison of District Ratings

Policy goal	Policy lever	Level of development				
		Kapuas	Manggarai Timur	Pacitan	Sukabumi	Sumbawa
Establishing an enabling environment	Legal framework	●●○○	●●○○	●●○○	●●○○	●●○○
	Coordination	●○○○	●○○○	●●○○	●●●○	●●●○
	Finance	●●●○	●●●○	●●●○	●●○○	●●○○
Implementing widely	Scope of programs	●●○○	●●○○	●●●○	●●●○	●●●●
	Coverage	●●○○	●●●○	●●●○	●●○○	●●○○
	Equity	●●○○	●○○○	●●●○	●●○○	●○○○
Monitoring and assuring quality	Data availability	●●○○	●●○○	●●○○	●●○○	●●○○
	Quality standards	●●●○	●●●○	●●●○	●●●○	●●●○
	Compliance with standards	●●○○	●●○○	●●●○	●●○○	●●●○

●○○○ Latent   ●●○○ Emerging   ●●●○ Established   ●●●● Advanced

delivered through various entry points. In addition, again for the districts that have not yet done so, it would be advisable to establish a district-level institutional anchor to coordinate ECD service delivery across sectors as delineated in the presidential decree. At first, the focus could be on information sharing and devising ways to enhance coordination, but as the anchor evolves and develops its capacity, it could assume a more strategic role in guiding the establishment of a holistic ECD district policy.

For a number of interventions, it would make sense to mandate universal coverage, or at least greatly expand coverage. This is the case for birth registration, which should be free, and where Pacitan has done better than other districts thanks to innovative programs. Many programs have limited coverage, and the priority should be to ensure access for children facing disadvantage, including orphans and children with special needs. Preprimary education should be expanded as participation in quality ECCE programs has been linked to improved attention and learning outcomes, as well as higher completion rates and school attainment levels. While a number of health interventions have good coverage, this is less the case for social protection and child protection services. In some of the districts especially, breastfeeding should be encouraged among new mothers, as exclusive breastfeeding until six months can reduce infant mortality and promote healthy development. Improvements in immunization requirements would also help.

For expanding various programs, higher budget allocations will often be required, and at least in some districts, the pay of service providers such as ECCE personnel should be improved. In addition, while some districts use explicit criteria and formulas for allocations of funds for early childhood programs across sectors, thereby ensuring more efficient and equitable allocation of resources, other districts have not yet adopted such practices.

On the data side, while good information is often available from administrative records and household surveys (including regular Demographic and Health Surveys) at the national and provincial level, this is not the case at the district level. Efforts are required here as well, including for tracking access to ECD programs and child-level outcomes in vulnerable groups. Many countries have developed simple tools to do so, such as child health and development passports. These types of data can help in identifying children in need of additional support. Monitoring compliance with quality standards—for construction as well as operation—through established accreditation procedures for ECCE facilities is also important. Resources need to be made available to preschool supervisors to properly monitor and support schools.

At district level, ECED supervisor (*Penilik*) is the one who, by Minister of State Apparatus and Bureaucracy Reform No. 14/2010, responsible for delivering quality assurance for ECED services. In most districts, however, the role of the supervisor in quality assurance does not work. It is therefore important for district as well as central government to revitalize the role of the supervisor in quality assurance. This can be done through capacity building for the supervisor, the development of tools, such as monitoring and evaluation tool to support them in the delivery of their role in quality assurance and better institutional and organizational supports for supervisor.

Table 4.7 provides a summary of district-level policy options for improved implementation. While some of these options are easily accessible and can be put into place fairly quickly and at low cost; others, also critically important, will take more time and investment of resources. Therefore, the policy options are classified into short- and medium-term options according to potentially required implementation timeframe.

Table 4.7 Summary of Policy Options to Improve ECD Implementation at the District Level

Short term (within 2 years)	Medium term (3–5 years)
1. Establishing an enabling environment	
Use explicit criteria and formulas for allocations of funds for early childhood programs across sectors ensuring more efficient and equitable allocation of resources. Such practices should be adopted across districts.	Consider implementing a HI-ECD policy at the district level. As a mandatory legal framework, the policy will guide the sectors at district level to provide HI-ECD services for all children.
Improve collaboration between district offices to ensure a comprehensive HI-ECD system beyond the education sector. Change the view that ECED is not only the role of education sector between district offices. HI-ECD measures the coordination within sectors and across institutions to deliver services effectively, including health and nutrition, as well as child and social protection sector.	Consider including the ECED sector into district annual educational development planning.

table continues next page

Table 4.7 Summary of Policy Options to Improve ECD Implementation at the District Level *(continued)*

Short term (within 2 years)	Medium term (3–5 years)
Strengthen communication between sectors (district offices). This could be done during annual joint meetings hosted by District Development Planning Agency.	Increase budget allocation to expand various programs. In at least some districts, this will involve improving salaries of service providers such as ECCE personnel and health workers.
Establish a district-level institutional anchor or joint secretariat to coordinate ECD service delivery across sectors. At first, the focus could be on information sharing and devising ways to enhance coordination, but as the anchor evolves and develops its capacity, it could assume a more strategic role in guiding the establishment of a holistic ECD district policy, as well as sharing cost.	
Encourage village participation in funding and provision of services. The issuance of Village Law No. 6/2014 provides broader opportunities for village governments to participate in funding and providing quality early childhood services through the village budget (*Anggaran Dana Desa*	

2. Implementing widely

Expand coverage of social protection and child protection services, which currently have lower coverage than health interventions. In some of the districts, breastfeeding should be encouraged to reduce infant mortality and promote healthy development.	Mandate universal coverage, or at least greatly expand coverage. For example, initiate a free-fee birth registration policy and provide low-cost services for disadvantaged children (poor families, live in rural or border areas, vulnerable and special needs children).
Improve immunization requirements.	

3. Monitoring and assuring quality

Track access to ECD programs and child-level outcomes in vulnerable groups. Many countries have developed simple tools to do so, such as child health and development passports. These types of data can help in identifying children in need of additional support.	Establish a one-source-data collection system for consistent use among district offices. It will help the mapping of children and their needs at district level.
Provide fee-free in-service training for early childhood teachers. Broaden access and enhance quality of in-service training (*Diklat Berjenjang*) to improve the quality of teachers.	Establish provincial- and district-level task forces to strengthen the accreditation system. It is sometimes difficult to get the accreditation from national level since it takes effort on cost and time.
	Improve compliance with quality standards—for construction as well as operation—through established accreditation procedures for ECCE facilities. Adequate resources need to be made available to preschool supervisors to properly monitor and support schools.

Note: ECCE = early childhood care and education; ECD = early childhood development; ECED = early childhood education and development; HI-ECD = Holistic Integrated-Early childhood development.

CHAPTER 5

SABER-ECD Ratings for Indonesia in Comparative Perspective

Amina Denboba and Quentin Wodon

Abstract

One of the objectives of the Systems Approach for Better Education Results (SABER) initiative is to produce comparable policy data between countries. Is the performance of Indonesia on the SABER Early Childhood Development (ECD) policy goals and levers at the level that would be expected for the country's level of economic development? To answer that question, it is necessary to document the relationship (or lack thereof) between ratings for various policy levers and goals and the level of economic development of countries, and next to locate where Indonesia stands with respect to that relationship. The objective of this chapter is to conduct this analysis using data from the implementation of SABER-ECD in 28 countries.

Introduction

One of the objectives of the SABER initiative is to produce comparable policy data between countries. While comparisons between Indonesia and a few other countries were provided in chapter 2 for some of indicators or ratings obtained for selected policy levers and goals, this was not done in a systematic way. In addition, these comparisons did not factor in (or control for) the level of development of countries. Using the data collected from the implementation of the SABER-ECD tool in 28 countries, this chapter provides an assessment of how well Indonesia is doing for each of the policy levers and goals in comparison to the expected level of performance of the country, given its level of economic development. In addition, the chapter provides a number of examples of best practice for each of the three policy goals of SABER-ECD.

The chapter is based on the analysis of SABER-ECD data collected for 28 countries: Albania, Armenia, Belize, Bulgaria, Colombia, The Gambia, Guinea,

---

The authors are very grateful to Janice Heejin Kim for research assistance.

Table 5.1 Comparative Performance of Indonesia for SABER-ECD Goals and Levers

	Goal 1: Enabling environment	Goal 2: Implementing widely	Goal 3: Ensuring quality	Lever 1: Legal framework	Lever 2: Coordination mechanism	Lever 3: Finance
Indonesia	3	2	2.5	3	3	3
Average	2.1	2.4	2.1	2.4	1.9	2.1

	Lever 4: Scope of programs	Lever 5: Coverage of programs	Lever 6: Equity in coverage	Lever 7: Data availability	Lever 8: Quality standards	Lever 9: Compliance with standards
Indonesia	3	2	2	3	2.9	1.7
Average	2.5	2.6	2.3	2.1	2.5	1.6

Source: World Bank SABER-ECD Survey.

Note: Each number indicates the level of development in early childhood development policy at the national level. "1" = latent, "2" = emerging, "3" = established, and "4" = advanced. Average indicates the average rating of 28 countries participated in the SABER-ECD Survey. SABER-ECD = Systems Approach for Better Education Results-Early Childhood Development.

Indonesia, Jamaica, Kyrgyz Republic, Malawi, Mauritius, Nepal, Nigeria, Samoa, Seychelles, Solomon Islands, Sri Lanka, Swaziland, Tajikistan, Tanzania, Togo, Tonga, Tuvalu, Uganda, Vanuatu, the Republic of Yemen, and Zanzibar. This sample includes low-income as well as middle-income countries. It turns out that in purchasing power parity (PPP)-adjusted US dollars, Indonesia is about at the midpoint of the sample of countries according to gross domestic product (GDP) per capita.

Table 5.1 provides the ratings for the various policy levers and goals obtained for Indonesia and for the full sample of countries on average. For two of the goals (establishing an enabling environment and ensuring quality), the performance of Indonesia is above that of the average for other countries where the tool has been implemented. For the third goal (implementing widely), Indonesia is performing less well. In terms of levers, Indonesia ranks above the average for seven levers and below for two (program coverage and equity), but these are particularly important levers in terms of services and interventions that actually reach households. The question is whether for its level of development, Indonesia has good policies.

The structure of the chapter is as follows: It first provides a simple analysis of the relationship between level of economic development and SABER-ECD ratings. It then provides examples of best practice for each of the three policy goals. A conclusion follows.

Ratings and Levels of Development

How closely related are the ratings for SABER-ECD policy levers and goals with the level of development of countries as measured by GDP per capita in current international $ (purchasing power parity-adjusted)[1] terms? Figure 5.1 as well as table 5.2 provide the answer. The figure provides simple scatter plots of the

Figure 5.1 Ratings in Policy Goals and Level of Development

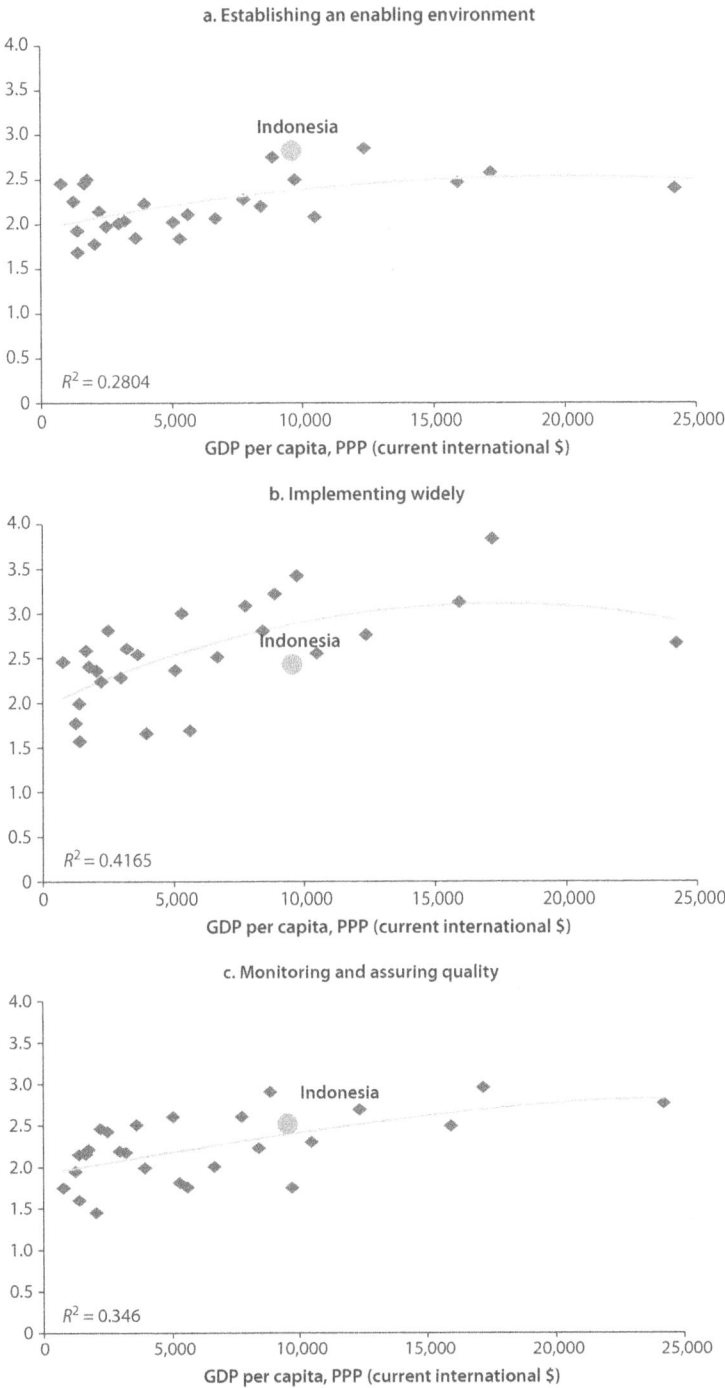

a. Establishing an enabling environment

b. Implementing widely

c. Monitoring and assuring quality

Source: World Bank SABER-ECD Survey.
Note: GDP = gross domestic product; PPP = purchasing power parity; SABER-ECD = Systems Approach for Better Education Results-Early Childhood Development.

Table 5.2 Relation between Policy Goals, Policy Levers, and Level of Development

Policy goals	Policy levers	R^2
1. Establishing an enabling environment		0.280
	Legal framework	0.092
	Intersectoral coordination	0.015
	Finance	0.473
2. Implementing widely		0.417
	Scope of programs	0.309
	Coverage	0.461
	Equity	0.279
3. Monitoring and assuring quality		0.346
	Data availability	0.260
	Quality standards	0.158
	Compliance with standards	0.283
Highest R^2	Finance	0.473
Lowest R^2	Intersectoral coordination	0.015

Source: World Bank SABER-ECD Survey.
Note: SABER-ECD = Systems Approach for Better Education Results-Early Childhood Development.

ratings of countries for policy goals on the vertical axis as a function of the level of economic development on the horizontal axis (similar figures are provided in annex at the level of policy levers). Table 5.2 provides the value of the R^2 of the regression line (or curve) traced through the scatter plots. A higher value for the R^2, which takes a value between 0 and 100 percent, denotes a closer association between the policy lever or goal rating and the level of development of countries.

Figure 5.1 (as well as the figures in annex 5A for policy goals) and table 5.2 suggest a strong correlation between ratings for finance (R^2 value of 0.473) and the rating for the coverage of programs (R^2 value of 0.461) and the level of economic development. This is not surprising since ensuring high coverage for key ECD interventions requires funding, and funding is more easily available among countries with higher levels of economic development. The correlations are smaller (R^2 values between 0.100 and 0.350) for the scope of programs and the equity in coverage, as well as the three policy levers for ensuring quality. The correlations are virtually zero (R^2 values below 0.100) for the last two policy levers: Legal framework and intersectoral coordination (R^2 values well below 0.05). In other words, countries at lower levels of economic development are rated, as well as countries at higher levels of economic development, for these two policy levers. As a result, the correlation between the first policy goal and economic development is the weakest, while the correlation between the second goal and economic development is the strongest.

In the various figures, the position of Indonesia is indicated by a large red dot. As mentioned earlier, for the first and third goals, Indonesia is above the average, and also above the expected level, given its GDP per capita. But for the second goal, which focuses on actual delivery of programs, Indonesia is performing below the average level and below the expected level for the country, given its GDP per capita.

Examples of International Best Practice

What are some examples of countries that have been performing very well in the various dimensions and that could provide inspiration for policy in Indonesia? This section provides illustrations of selected best practice policies for all three policy goals from around the world, including a few countries where the SABER-ECD tool has been applied (Jamaica and Mauritius).

Establishing an Enabling Environment

In the case of the first policy goal—establishing an enabling environment, at least four experiences can be mentioned. First, in Chile, a holistic ECD system is embedded in the law, guaranteeing differentiated support for the poorest 40 percent of children. In 2005, the Government of Chile embarked on an ambitious path to improve ECD, which culminated in September 2009 with the *Chile Crece Contigo* (CCC, Chile Grows with you) Law No. 20,379. CCC is an intersectoral and multidisciplinary approach to achieve high-quality ECD by protecting children from conception onwards with relevant and timely services that provide opportunities for early stimulation and development. A core element of the system is that it provides differentiated support and guarantees for boys and girls from the poorest 40 percent of households, including free access to preprimary school. Furthermore, the CCC mandates provision of services for orphans and vulnerable children and children with special needs. The creation and implementation of the CCC has been accomplished through a multisectoral, highly synergetic approach at all levels of government. At the central level, the Presidential Council is responsible for the development, planning, and budgeting of the program. At each of the national, regional, provincial, and local levels, there are institutional bodies tasked with supervision and support, operative action, as well as development, planning, and budgeting for each respective level. Other pertinent aspects of the Chilean Social System is 18 weeks of paid maternity leave and additional 4 days of paid leave for fathers, both of which are high by Latin American standards. The legal framework includes mandatory iron fortification of food staples and salt iodization and promotion of the International Code of Marketing of Break Milk Substitute.

Second, in Jamaica in 2003, the government established the Early Childhood Commission (ECC) as an official agency to govern the administration of ECD in Jamaica (Early Childhood Commission Act). Operating under the Ministry of Education, the ECC is responsible for advising the Ministry of Education on ECD policy matters. It assists in the preparation as well as monitoring and evaluation of ECD plans and programs, acts as a coordinating agency to streamline ECD activities, manages the national ECD budget, and supervises and regulates early childhood institutions. The ECC includes a governance arm comprising the officially appointed Executive Director, a Board of Commissioners, and seven subcommittees representing governmental and nongovernmental organizations. It also has an operational arm that provides support to the board and subcommittees. The ECC is designed with representation from all relevant sectors, including education, health, local government and community development, labor, finance, protection, and planning. Each ministry or government agency nominates a representative to serve on the Board of Commissioners. The seven subcommittees which provide technical support to the ECC board comprise 50 governmental and nongovernmental agencies. Furthermore, the newly established National Parenting Support Commission creates links between Jamaican parents and the Government of Jamaica. In 2012, the Ministry of Education introduced the National Parenting Support Policy. The government recognized that parents should serve an important role to promote and coordinate organizational efforts and resources for positive parenting practices. The National Parenting Support Commission Act further established an official coordinating body to ensure effective streamlining of government activities related to parenting.

Third, in Australia a participatory approach was used to achieve universal preprimary education and develop the ECD strategy, with the strategy now embedded in a strong legal framework. The Council of Australian Governments created the National Partnership Agreement on Early Childhood Education, which commits the Commonwealth and State and Territory Governments to ensure that all children have access to a quality early childhood education program in the year preceding formal schooling by 2013. The program is required to be delivered by a four-year university-trained early childhood teacher and be provided for a minimum of 15 hours a week, 40 weeks per year. Developed under the auspices of the Council of Australian Governments in 2009, Investing in the Early Years—A National Early Childhood Development Strategy is a joint effort to ensure that by 2020 all children have the best start in life to create a better future for them and for the nation. The strategy is a comprehensive approach to ECD that focuses on a child's life cycle, across the four interrelated dimensions of ECD, from the prenatal period to age eight. An important factor for emphasis in Australia's establishment of a comprehensive ECD system has been the effective participation, cooperation, and policy development across all levels of government. The strategy acknowledges that families, community, organizations, workplace, and government all play critical roles in shaping children's development and thus requires an effective ECD system with sufficient capacity and stakeholder synergy.

Fourth, related to financing, Mauritius has developed a conditional cash transfer program to increase preprimary enrollment. To encourage parents to enroll their children, the government provides all families with financial support contingent upon the child attending the final year of preprimary school (age four years in Mauritius). The transfer amounts to $6 per month and has helped achieve an 85 percent enrollment rate in preprimary school for children ages three to five years in Mauritius. Provision is largely through nonstate centers (17 percent of all preschools are state managed), but the design and enforcement of quality control mechanisms has remained central to government policy efforts.

Implementing Widely

For the second policy goal—implementing widely, the experiences of France and Sweden can be considered as best practice. Early childhood strategies in France aim to (1) increase childcare facilities and support; (2) increase benefits to provide partial cover of the cost of child care by registered and accredited child minders; and (3) provide generous paid parental leave for parents who withdraw from the labor market. Publicly funded early childhood education (ECE) is well established and has a long history in France. Since the 1980s, ECE is the embedded under the auspices of the Ministry of Education. Children have a legal right to a place in a preschool from the age of three years. France has one of the highest levels of publicly funded universal ECE provision amongst the EU countries for children ages three to five years. France invests considerably in childcare and education services in the years preceding formal school entry and has achieved remarkable success in terms of providing equal opportunities for children. The *ecole maternelle* is the dominant institutional form of ECE provision for children ages three years to school entry age, providing a full-day service throughout the school year. Alongside the *ecoles maternelles*, there are a number of other forms of services outside the education system, particularly for children younger than three years of age, administered under the joint responsibility of the Ministry of Employment, Social Cohesion and Housing, and the Ministry of Health and Solidarity. Publicly subsidized centre-based services include childcare centers (*etablissements d'accueil regulier*), parent cooperatives (*etablissements a gestion parentale*), multicare (*multi-acceuil*), and 'kindergartens' (*jardins d'enfants*) providing flexible childcare services. Family daycare (*Assistance maternelle*) and family crèche (*service d'accueil familial*) are other forms of childcare provision for children under three. Furthermore, a number of other innovative services have been established with the aim to provide equitable access in rural and urban areas, including mobile services (*services itinerants*) and open door services (*lieux d'accueil enfants parents*).

Preschool educators (*professeurs des ecoles*) are generally trained at the same level and in the same training institutions as primary teachers, and caregivers within the social welfare system are primarily trained in the paramedical and health care domain. France provides generous family benefits allowing parents to choose the type of childcare facility they think best for their child and to reduce their professional activities in order to devote themselves to their child's education. The *Prestation d'Accueil du Jeune Enfant* was introduced as a unified early childhood benefit system through the *Caisses d'Allocation Familiale* and includes monthly benefits from the seventh month of pregnancy until the child reaches age three. This benefit system is correlated with the child's health care, thus child medical visits are required in order for the parents to be able to receive any benefit.

In Sweden, young children benefit from a continuum of ECD services from birth to age six years. A unique and effective feature of this system is the multitude of options from which parents can choose. High-quality early childhood education is a legal right for all children. The three differentiated education interventions are preschool; family daycare homes; and, open preschools. Preschool, which operates year-round and provides a minimum of 525 hours of schooling, accommodates 15–20 students per class and accounts for the majority of children enrolled in ECE, including 92.7 percent of four-year-olds, 93 percent of five-year-olds, and 95.1 percent of six-year-olds. Family daycare homes, which are registered providers, are available to children ages 1–12 years. Approximately 4.3 percent of one- to five-year-olds attend, the larger portion of whom being located in rural areas. Open preschools service children ages one to seven years and actively involve the parent in the classroom. Health care services are free of charge for all pregnant mothers and children ages five years and younger. Services are mostly provided through maternal care centers and childcare centers and include pre- and postnatal care, routine health check-ups, hearing, sight, and other developmental screening. In addition, children receive free immunizations and dental health services. Coverage levels are near universal. Sweden's ECD system achieves high-level equity, including full integration of children with disabilities and special needs. There is very little disparity in terms of access to ECD services by socioeconomic status, or by rural and urban localities, because of the free provision of services and the diversity of services offered.

Monitoring and Assuring Quality

For the third policy goal—monitoring and assuring quality—the experiences of New Zealand, Sweden, and Jamaica can be considered as best practice. The government of New Zealand has recognized that the establishment of an effective ECD system requires extensive information on both the current state of child development in the country, as well as the establishment of standard measures to guide a child's development. Most ECD-related interventions have devised frameworks to monitor and evaluate the impact and efficacy of interventions. As such, the government of New Zealand has invested heavily in the development of quality assurance frameworks and mechanisms to ensure ECD services effectively contribute to the development of children.

In the education sector, the integration of childcare services under the auspices of the Ministry of Education has been a crucial step for the development of quality early childhood care and education (ECCE) services. As a result of this integration, New Zealand is one of the first countries in the world to develop an innovative national early childhood education curriculum—The New Zealand Curriculum for English medium (NZC) and *Te Marautange o Aotearoa* for Maori medium (TMoA)—covering the entire age range from birth to five years. National Standards have been established to set the direction for teaching and learning in New Zealand schools, providing teachers with clear learning goals, guidance and information about students' progress as they develop local curriculum and engaging contexts for the learning needs of their students. The ministry has further developed a strategic framework for generating good information about the implementation and outcomes of National Standards: the Ministry's Pathways to the Future: *Nga Huauahi Arataki*, a 10-Year Strategic Plan for Early Childhood Education, sets improving quality as one of its main goals. Innovative approaches have been developed to assess children's experiences and for teachers' self-evaluation. The Ministry of Education considers the health, safety, and well-being of children in early childhood education services of utmost importance. The Education Regulations 2008 set out a range of requirements to which all ECE must adhere. This affected health and safety issues, staffing (ratios and qualifications), resources, facilities, and program delivery. The framework will draw from a range of different and complementary information sources, which will contribute to ministry decision making on ongoing implementation and support for the standards. The ministry has also undertaken numerous internal and external reviews of the ECE sector, which have been valuable tools for informing policy. The integration has resulted in substantial increase of quality assurance between different types of ECCE services.

Throughout the life of Well Child Services, the government and the Ministry of Health have undertaken numerous reviews as part of their ongoing commitment to child health. The most recent was completed in 2010, and restructured many aspects of Well Child Services. One noteworthy change is the development of an evidence-based quality framework that works to ensure the program consistently achieves positive outcomes for all participating children and their families. A National Immunization Register records immunization events. In addition to specific research exercises that pertain to individual interventions or sectors, ongoing endeavors are being undertaken to contribute to the wealth of knowledge of childhood development in New Zealand. These activities help inform policy makers, intervention operators, and communities and families. Led by the University of Auckland, and with financial contributions from multiple government agencies, Growing up in New Zealand is a longitudinal study of children and families that follows a group of 7,000 children from the time they were born until they become adults. This is the first such study of its kind in New Zealand. The objective is to gain a better understanding of raising happy, healthy children, and, ultimately, to use this information to make more informed decisions that will improve the lives of all New Zealand children. It will be a number of years before its yields valuable information. The Ministry of Social Development (MoSD) consults with social agencies within the health, care and support, education, economic security, safety, civil and political rights, justice, cultural identity, social connectedness, and environment domains to produce Publications of Children and Young People: Indicators of Wellbeing in New Zealand. The second report was realized in 2008 and provides insight on the status of New Zealand children and young people. The NSU monitors the quality of screening programs and works with expert groups and consumers to ensure that each screening program is based on the latest evidence and meets high standards. All providers are required to meet the professional, ethical and legal standards set by the UNHSPIP National Policy and Quality Standards.

In Sweden, an articulated curriculum, central monitoring, and quality assurance framework help improve local service delivery. ECD policies, objectives, and overall framework are set at the central level. Local governments are empowered to operate interventions in response to local demands and characteristics, thus providing services that are more context specific. Depending on the intervention, quality assurance mechanisms can take different forms and, in some instances, a multipronged approach is suitable. This is best evidenced through the preschool system where the Swedish Schools Inspectorate ensures compliance by conducting inspections of facilities to oversee and examine the quality of schools, while the National Agency for Education is responsible for facilitating and ensuring proper use of state funding and grants. In July 2011, Sweden adopted a revised curriculum. The main enhancement is the better articulation of the pedagogical tasks of the preschool system by clarifying the goals for language and communication, mathematics, natural science, and technology. The centers are autonomous to evolve their own local curricula and pedagogical methods from the principles outlined in the state curriculum. The National Agency for Education publishes supporting material and general guidelines with comments for guidance and supervision. In conjunction with the preschool system, the Universal Health Care System schedule presents a systematic approach to checkups, child evaluations, and interventions to ensure the needs of all young children are monitored and met across the four interrelated dimensions of ECD.

Jamaica has established standards and compliance mechanisms to assure quality in early childhood institutions. The Early Childhood Commission (ECC) was established by an Act of Parliament, the Early Childhood Commission Act, in 2003. The Commission has the responsibility to ensure the integrated and coordinated delivery of early childhood programs and services. Through its varying activities, the ECC will guide the holistic development of children, including physical, cognitive, social, and emotional development. The Commission has a range of legislated functions, one of which indicates direct responsibility to supervise and regulate early childhood institutions.

Standards for the operation, management, and administration of early childhood institutions are in place. In Jamaican law, there are two types of standards: those transmitted by an Act or Regulations and which therefore carry legal consequences and those that serve to improve practice voluntarily and are not legally binding. For practical purposes, quality standards for early childhood institutions include both sets of standards, with clear indications of those standards that are legally binding. To improve the quality of services provided by early childhood institutions, the ECC has developed a range of robust operational quality standards for early childhood institutions. The Act and Regulations, which together comprise the legal requirements, specify the minimum levels of practice below which institutions will not be registered or allowed to operate.

The standards that are not legally binding define best practices for early childhood institutions and serve to encourage institutions to raise their level of practice above minimum requirements. While early childhood institutions are encouraged to achieve the highest possible standards to ensure the best outcomes for children, the legally binding standards guarantee that minimum standards are met.

Inspection and registration frameworks are in place. Inspection of early childhood institutions is the procedure designated under the Early Childhood Act for ensuring that operators comply with the minimum acceptable standards of practice. The ECC is required to inspect each early childhood institution twice annually. It is a requirement of registration that the registered operator cooperates with the ECC's inspection process. The "registered operator" is defined as the person required to apply for registration of an early childhood institution and may be an individual or a group. In deciding on the suitability of an early childhood institution for registration under the Early Childhood Act, the ECC will, based on information obtained at inspection visits, determine whether or not an early childhood institution meets and complies with the Act and Regulations. Where existing provision falls short of the legal requirements, and the shortfall does not present a real and present danger to children, a permit to operate until full requirements are met will be granted, with time scales for institutions to meet requirements. The ECC encourages the promotion of the highest standards of practice by monitoring not only the minimum requirements at inspection visits but also those standards that are not legally binding.

Conclusion

The SABER initiative aims to produce comparable policy data between countries on policies implemented in various domains. In the case of SABER-ECD, data have been collected in 28 countries. This chapter has provided an assessment of how well Indonesia is doing for each of the nine policy levers and three policy goals of SABER-ECD in comparison to the expected level of performance of the country computed from the multicountry dataset, given Indonesia's level of economic development. In addition, the chapter provided a number of examples of best practice policies implemented by countries for each of the three policy goals of SABER-ECD.

Overall, for two of the SABER-ECD goals (establishing an enabling environment and ensuring quality), the performance of Indonesia is above that of the average for other countries where the tool has been implemented and also above the expected level of performance of the country, given its level of GDP per capita. But for the third goal (implementing widely), Indonesia is performing less well than it should. This is important because at the end of the game what matters most for ECD is that essential interventions indeed reach young children.

Note

1. GDP per capita based on purchasing power parity (PPP). PPP GDP is gross domestic product converted to international dollars using purchasing power parity rates. An international dollar has the same purchasing power over GDP as the U.S. dollar has in the United States.

Annex 5A: Ratings and Level of Economic Development for Policy Goals

Figure A5.1   Ratings in Policy Levers and Level of Development

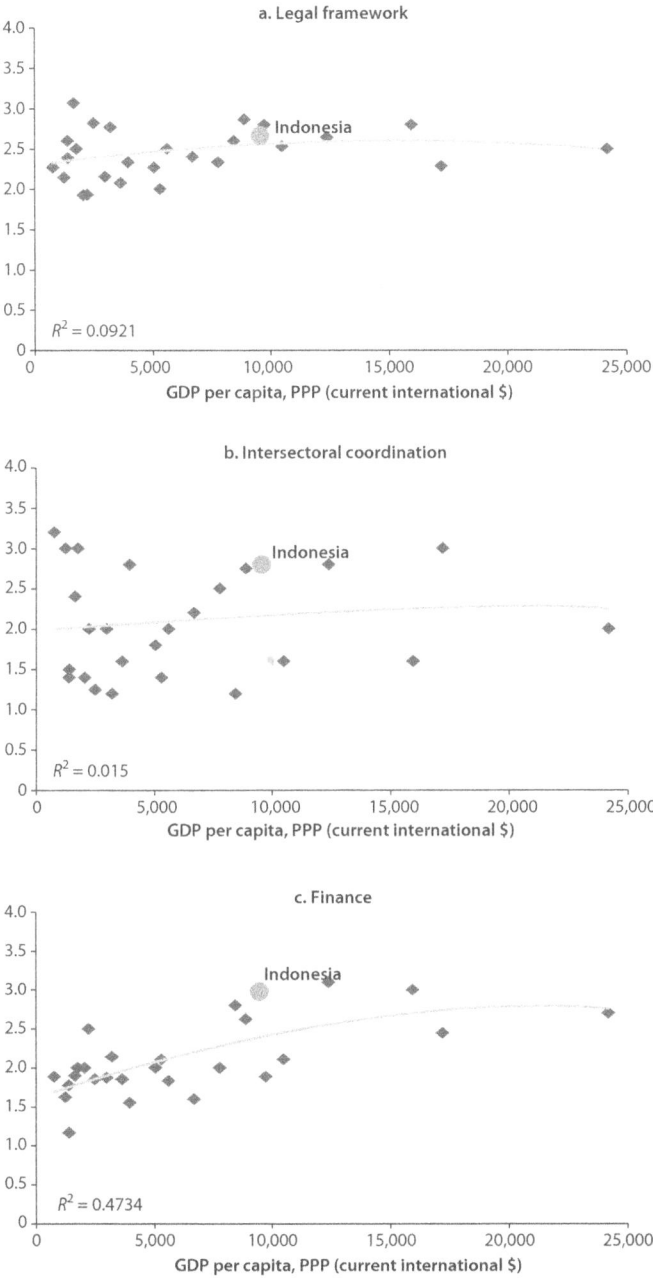

a. Legal framework

$R^2 = 0.0921$

GDP per capita, PPP (current international $)

b. Intersectoral coordination

$R^2 = 0.015$

GDP per capita, PPP (current international $)

c. Finance

$R^2 = 0.4734$

GDP per capita, PPP (current international $)

Source: World Bank SABER-ECD Survey.
Note: GDP = gross domestic product; PPP = purchasing power parity; SABER-ECD = Systems Approach for Better Education Results-Early Childhood Development.

Figure A5.1   Ratings in Policy Levers and Level of Development *(continued)*

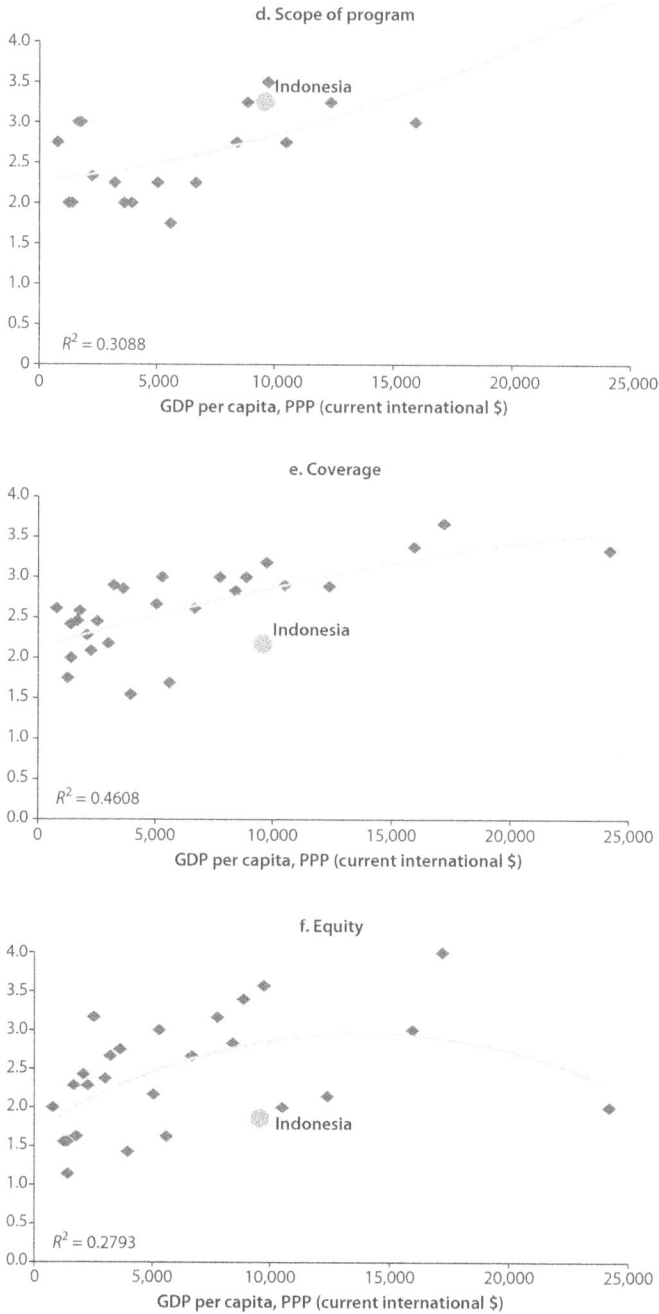

d. Scope of program

$R^2 = 0.3088$

GDP per capita, PPP (current international $)

e. Coverage

$R^2 = 0.4608$

GDP per capita, PPP (current international $)

f. Equity

$R^2 = 0.2793$

GDP per capita, PPP (current international $)

Source: World Bank SABER-ECD Survey.
Note: GDP = gross domestic product; PPP = purchasing power parity; SABER-ECD = Systems Approach for Better Education Results-Early Childhood Development.

Figure A5.1   Ratings in Policy Levers and Level of Development *(continued)*

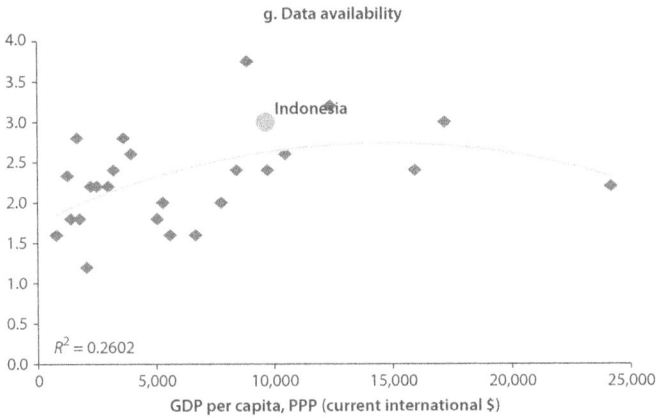

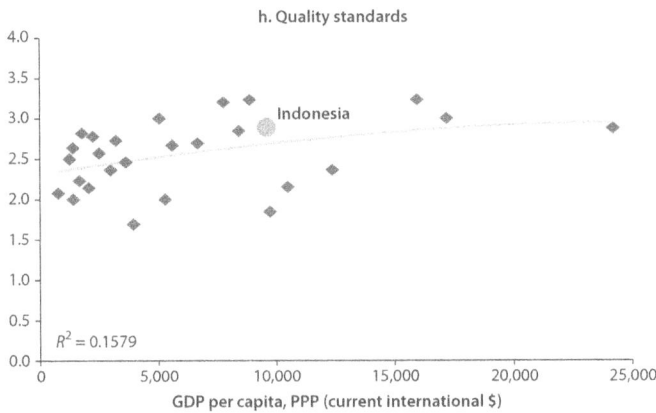

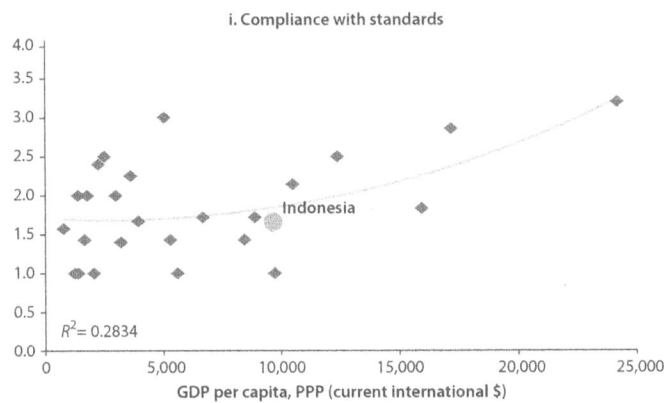

g. Data availability

h. Quality standards

i. Compliance with standards

Source: World Bank SABER-ECD Survey.
Note: GDP = gross domestic product; PPP = purchasing power parity; SABER-ECD = Systems Approach for Better Education Results-Early Childhood Development.

References

Abadzi, H. 2006. *Efficient Learning for the Poor: Insights from the Frontier of Cognitive Neuroscience*. Washington, DC: World Bank.

Aboud, F., and S. Akhter. 2011. "A Cluster-randomized Evaluation of a Responsive Stimulation and Feeding Intervention in Bangladesh." *Pediatrics* 127 (5): 1191–7.

Alderman, H., eds. 2011. *No Small Matter: The Impact of Poverty, Shocks and Human Capital Investments in Early Childhood Development*. Washington, DC: World Bank.

Alderman, H., L. Elder, A. Goyal, A. Herforth, Y. T. Hoberg, A. Marini, J. Ruel-Bergeron, J. Saavedra, M. Shekar, and S. Tiwari. 2013. *Improving Nutrition through Multisectoral Approaches*. Washington, DC: World Bank.

Arnold, C., K. Bartlett, S. Gowani, and R. Merali. 2006. "Is Everybody Ready? Readiness, Transition and Continuity: Reflections and Moving Forward." Paper Commissioned for the EFA Global Monitoring Report 2007, UNESCO, Paris.

Arnold, C., K. Bartlett, S. Gowani, and S. Shallwani. 2008. "Transition to School: Reflections on Readiness." *Journal of Developmental Processes* 3 (2): 26–38.

Baltussen, R., C. Knai, and M. Sharan. 2004. "Iron Fortification and Iron Supplementation Are Cost-Effective Interventions to Reduce Iron Deficiency in Four Subregions of the World." *Journal of Nutrition* 134: 2678–84.

Barnighausen, T., D. Bloom, D. Canning, A. Friedman, O. Levine, J. O'Brien, L. Privor-Dumm, and D. Walker. 2009. Copenhagen Consensus: Best Practice Paper: The Economic Case for Expanding Vaccination Coverage of Children. http://www.copen-hagenconsensus.com.

Barrientos, A., J. Byrne, J. M. Villa, and P. Peña. 2013. "Social Transfers and Child Protection." Office of Research Working Paper, UNICEF, New York.

Bentley, M. E., S. Vazir, P. Engle, N. Balakrishna, S. L. Johnson, H. Creed, P. L. Griffiths, and S. Fernandez-Rao. 2010. "A Home-based Educational Intervention to Caregivers in South India to Improve Complementary Feeding and Responsive Feeding, and Psychosocial Stimulation Increases Dietary Intake, Growth and Development of Infants." *The FASEB Journal* 24 (suppl): 564.14.

Bhutta, Z., J. Das, A. Rizvi, M. Gaffey, N. Walker, S. Horton, P. Webb, A. Lartey, R. Black, and the Maternal and Child Undernutrition Group. 2013. "Evidence-based Interventions for Improvement of Maternal and Child Nutrition: What Can Be Done and At What Cost?" *The Lancet* 382 (9890): 452–77.

Bhutta, Z., T. Ahmed, R. Black, S. Cousens, K. Dewey, E. Giugliani, B. Haider, B. Kirkwood, S. Morris, H. Sachdev, and M. Shekar. 2008. "What Works? Interventions for Maternal and Child Undernutrition and Survival." *The Lancet* 371 (9610): 417–40.

Black, R. E., C. G. Victora, S. P. Walker, and the Maternal and Child Nutrition Study Group. 2013. "Maternal and Child Undernutrition and Overweight in Low-income and Middle-income Countries." *The Lancet* 382 (9890): 427–51.

Brinkerhoff, D. W. 2004. "The Enabling Environment for Implementing the Millennium Development Goals: Government Actions to Support NGOs." In Proceedings of the George Washington University Conference: The Role of NGOs in Implementing the Millennium Development Goals, Washington, DC, USA, May 6–7.

Britto, P. R., H. Yoshikawa, and K. Boller. 2011. "Quality of Early Childhood Development Programs: Rationale for Investment, Conceptual Framework and Implications for Equity." *Social Policy Report* 25 (2):1–31.

Britto, P. R., P. Engle, and S. Super, eds. 2013. *Handbook of Early Childhood Development Research and Its Impact on Global Policy*. New York, NY: Oxford University Press.

Bryce, J., S. el Arifeen, G. Pariyo, C. F. Lanata, D. Gwatkin, J.-P. Habicht, and the Multi-Country Evaluation of Imci Study Group. 2003. "Reducing Child Mortality: Can Public Health Deliver?" *The Lancet* 362: 159–64.

Cairncross, S., C. Hunt, S. Boisson, K. Bostoen, V. Curtis, I. Fung, and W. Schmidt. 2010. "Water, Sanitation and Hygiene for the Prevention of Diarrhea." *International Journal of Epidemiology* 39 (suppl 1): i193–205.

Ching, P., M. Birmingham, T. Goodman, R. Sutter, and B. Loevinsohn. 2000. "Childhood Mortality Impact and Costs of Integrating Vitamin A Supplementation into Immunization Campaigns." *American Journal of Public Health* 90 (10): 1526–9.

Consultative Group on Early Childhood Care and Development. 1991. *Preparing Children for Schools and Schools for Children*. New York: UNICEF.

Currie, J., and D. Thomas. 1999. "Early Test Scores, Socioeconomic Status and Future Outcomes." NBER Working Paper 6943, National Bureau of Economic Research, Cambridge, MA.

Denboba, A., R. Sayre, Q. Wodon, L. Elder, L. Rawlings, and J. Lombardi. 2014. *Stepping Up Early Childhood Development: Investing in Young Children with High Returns*. Washington, DC: World Bank.

Dillingham, R., and R. L. Guerrant. 2004. "Childhood Stunting: Measuring and Stemming the Staggering Costs of Inadequate Water and Sanitation." The *Lancet* 363 (9403): 94–5.

Engle, P. L., L. C. H. Fernald, H. Alderman, J. Behrman, C. O'Gara, A. Yousafzai, M. Cabral de Mello, M. Hidrobo, N. Ulkuer, and the Global Child Development Steer Group. 2011. "Strategies for Reducing Inequalities and Improving Developmental Outcomes for Young Children in Low-income and Middle-income Countries." *The Lancet* 378 (9799): 1339–53.

Engle, P. L., L. C. H. Fernald, H. Alderman, J. Behrman, C. O'Gara, A. Yousafzai, M. Cabral de Mello, M. Hidrobo, N. Ulkuer, and the Global Child Development Steer Group. 2011. "Strategies for Reducing Inequalities and Improving Developmental Outcomes for Young Children in Low-income and Middle-income Countries." *The Lancet* Early Online Publication, September 23. doi:10.1016/S0140–6736(11) 60889–1.

Esrey, A. 1996. "Water, Waste, and Well-being: A Multi-country Study." *American Journal of Epidemiology* 143 (6): 608.

Esrey, S. A., J. B. Potash, L. Roberts, and C. Shiff. 1991. "Effects of Improved Water Supply and Sanitation on Ascariasis, Diarrhoea, Dracunculiasis, Hookworm Infection,

Schistosomiasis, and Trachoma." *Bulletin of the World Health Organization* 69 (5): 609–21.

Fabian, H., and A. W. Dunlop. 2007. "Outcomes of Good Practice in Transition Processes for Children Entering Primary School." Working Paper 42, Bernard van Leer Foundation, The Hague, Netherlands.

Fay, M., D. Leipziger, Q. Wodon, and T. Yepes. 2005. "Achieving Child-Health-Related Millennium Development Goals: The Role of Infrastructure." *World Development* 33 (8): 1267–84.

Feinstein, L. 2003. "Inequality in the Early Cognitive Development of British Children in the 1970 Cohort." *Economica* 70 (1): 73–97.

Fiedler, J. L. 2000. "The Nepal National Vitamin A Program: Prototype to Emulate or Donor Enclave?" *Health Policy and Planning* 15 (2): 145–56.

Grantham-McGregor, S., S. Walker, S. Chang, and C. Powell. 1997. "Effects of Early Childhood Supplementation With and Without Stimulation on Later Development in Stunted Jamaican Children." *American Journal of Clinical Nutrition* 66: 247–53.

Grantham-McGregor, S., Y. Bun Cheung, S. Cueto, P. Glewwe, L. Richer, B. Trupp, and the International Child Development Steering Group. 2007. "Developmental Potential in the First 5 Years for Children in Developing Countries." *The Lancet* 369 (9555): 60–70.

Greenberg, J. 2011. *The Impact of Maternal Education on Children's Enrollment in Early Childhood Education and Care*. New York: Lehman College/CUNY.

Hanushek, E. A., and D. D. Kimko. 2000. "Schooling, Labor-Force Quality, and the Growth of Nations." *The American Economic Review* 90 (5): 1184–208.

Hanushek, E. A., and J. A. Luque. 2003. "Efficiency and Equity in Schools around the World." *Economics of Education Review, Elsevier* 22 (5): 481–502, October.

Hasan, Amer, Marilou Hyson, and Mae Chu Chang, eds. 2013. *Early Childhood Education and Development in Poor Villages of Indonesia: Strong Foundations, Later Success*. Directions in Development. Washington, DC: World Bank.

Heckman, J. J., and D. V. Masterov. 2007. "The Productivity Argument for Investing in Young Children." *Applied Economic Perspectives and Policy* 29 (3): 446–93.

Heckman, J. J., S. H. Moon, R. Pinto, P. A. Savalyev, and A. Yavitz. 2009. "The Rate of Return to the High/Scope Perry Preschool Program." Working Paper 200936, Geary Institute, University College Dublin.

Heejin Kim, J., and Q. Wodon. 2015. *Coverage of Essential ECD Interventions in Indonesia*. Washington, DC: World Bank.

Heymann, J., A. Raub, and A. Earle. 2011. "Creating and Using New Data Sources to Analyze the Relationship between Social Policy and Global Health: The Case of Maternal Leave." *Public Health Reports* 126 (3): 127–34.

Horton, S. 1992. "United Costs, Cost-Effectiveness, and Financing of Nutrition Interventions." HNP Working Paper No. 952, World Bank, Washington, DC.

Horton, S., and J. Ross. 2003. "The Economics of Iron Deficiency." *Food Policy* 28 (1): 51–75.

Horton, S., H. Alderman, and J. Rivera. 2008. Copenhagen Consensus 2008 Challenge Paper: Hunger and Malnutrition. http://www.copenhagenconsensus.com.

Horton, S., M. Shekar, C. McDonald, A. Mahal, and J. K. Brooks. 2010. *Scaling up Nutrition: What Will It Cost?* Washington, DC: World Bank.

Hotez, P. J., D. A. Bundy, K. Beegle, S. Brooker, L. Drake, N. D. Silva, A. Montresor, D. Engels, M. Jukes, L. Chitsulo, J. Chow, R. Laxminarayan, C. M. Michaud, J. Bethony, O. Correa, X. Shu Hua, A. Fenwick, and L. Savioli. 2006. "Helminth Infections: Soil Transmitted Helminth Infections and Schistosomiasis." In *Disease Control Priorities in Developing Countries.* 2nd ed. Washington, DC: World Bank and Oxford University Press.

Hutton, G., and L. Haller. 2004. *Evaluation of the Costs and Benefits of Water and Sanitation Improvements at the Global level.* Geneva: World Health Organization.

Immervoll, H., and D. Barber. 2005. "Can Parents Afford to Work?: Childcare Costs, Tax-Benefit Policies and Work Incentives." OECD Social, Employment and Migration Working Paper No. 31, OECD Publishing, Paris.

International Labour Organization. 2010. *Workplace Solutions for Childcare.* Geneva: International Labour Organization.

Jalan, J., and M. Ravallion. 2003. "Does Piped Water Reduce Diarrhea for Children in Rural India?" *Journal of Econometrics* 112: 153–73.

Janus, M., and D. Offord. 2000. "Readiness to Learn at School." *ISUMA* 1 (2): 71–5.

Kosek, M., C. Bern, and L. R. Guerrant. 2003. "The Global Burden of Diarrheal Disease, As Estimated from Studies Published between 1992 and 2000." *Bulletin of the World Health Organization* 81: 197–204.

Landry, S., K. Smith, and P. Swank. 2006. Responsive Parenting: Establishing Early Foundations for Social, Communication, and Independent Problem-solving Skills." *Developmental Psychology* 42 (4): 627–42.

Laxminarayan, R., J. Chow, and S. A. Shahid-Salles. 2006. "Intervention Cost-Effectiveness: Overview of Main Messages." In *Disease Control Priorities in Developing Countries.* 2nd ed., edited by D. T. Jamison, J. G. Breman, A. R. Measham, G. Alleyne, M. Claeson, D. B. Evans, P. Jha, A. Mills, and P. Musgrove. Washington, DC: World Bank.

Lombardi, J., A. Mosle, N. Patel, R. Schumacher, and J. Stedron. 2014. *Gateways to Two Generations: The Potential for Early Childhood Programs and Partnerships to Support Children and Parents Together.* Washington, DC: Aspen Institute.

Ministry of Education. 2012. *Buku Data PAUDNI, 2012.* Jakarta.

Ministry of Women Empowerment and Child Protection and Central Bureau of Statistics. 2012. Profile of Indonesian Children. 2012. Jakarta. http://www.kemenpppa.go.id/index.php/daftar-buku/profil-anak?download=510%3Aprofilanak2012.

Moe, C. L., and R. D. Rheingans. 2006. "Global Challenges in Water, Sanitation and Health." *Journal of Water and Health* 4: 41.

Myers, R., and C. Landers. 1989. "Preparing Children for Schools and Schools for Children." Discussion paper prepared for the fifth meeting of the Consultative Group on Early Childhood Care and Development, UNESCO, Paris.

Naudeau, S., N. Kataoka, A. Valerio, M. J. Neuman, and L. K. Elder. 2011. *Investing in Young Children: An Early Childhood Development Guide for Policy Dialogue and Project Preparation.* Washington, DC: World Bank.

Naudeau, S., N. Kataoka, A. Valerio, M. J. Neuman, and L. K. Elder. 2011. *Investing in Young Children: An Early Childhood Development Guide for Policy Dialogue and Project Preparation.* Directions in Development. Washington, DC: World Bank.

Nelson, C. 2007. "A Neurobiological Perspective on Early Human Deprivation." *Child Development Perspectives* 1 (1): 13–18.

Neuman, M. J. 2007. "Good Governance of Early Childhood Care and Education: Lessons from the 2007 *Education for All Global Monitoring Report*." UNESCO Policy Briefs on Early Childhood. United Nations Educational, Scientific, and Cultural Organization, New York.

Neuman, M. J., and A. E. Devercelli. 2013. "What Matters Most for Early Childhood Development: A Framework Paper." SABER Working Paper Series, World Bank, Washington, DC.

Neuman, M., and A. Devercelli. 2013. *"What Matters Most for Early Childhood Development: A Framework Paper."* SABER, Washington, DC: World Bank.

Neuman, M., and A. Devercelli. 2013. "What Matters Most for Early Childhood Development: A Framework Paper." SABER, World Bank, Washington DC

Neuman, M., and A. Devercelli. 2013. *Investing Early: Matters Most for Early Childhood Development: A Framework Paper.* Washington, DC: World Bank.

Neuman, Michelle J., and Amanda E. Devercelli. 2013. "What Matters Most for Early Childhood Development: A Framework Paper." SABER, World Bank, Washington, DC.

OECD (Organisation for Economic Co-operation and Development). 2011. *Starting Strong III: A Quality Toolbox for Early Childhood Education and Care.* Paris: OECD Publications.

Pianta, R., K. LaParo, and B. Hamre. 2007. *Classroom Assessment Scoring System—CLASS.* Baltimore: Brookes.

Reynolds, A. J., J. A. Temple, D. L. Robertson, and E. A. Mann. 2001. "Long Term Effects of an Early Childhood Intervention on Educational Achievement and Juvenile Arrest- a 15- Year Follow-Up of Low-Income Children in Public Schools." *Journal of the American Medical Association* 285 (18): 2339–46.

Rijsberman, F., and A. P. Zwane. 2012. Copenhagen Consensus 2012 Challenge Paper: Water and Sanitation. http://www.copenhagenconsensus.com.

Robberstad, B., T. Strand, R. E. Black, and H. Sommerfelt. 2004. "Cost-Effectiveness of Zinc as Adjunct Therapy for Acute Childhood Diarrhea in Developing Countries." *Bulletin of the World Health Organization* 82 (7): 523–31.

Rolnick, A. J., and R. Grunewald. 2007. "The Economics of Early Childhood Development as Seen by Two Fed Economists." *Community Investments* 19 (2): 13–30. Federal Reserve Bank of San Francisco.

Ruel, M., H. Alderman, and the Maternal and Child Undernutrition Group. 2013. "Nutrition-Sensitive Interventions and Programmes: How Can They Help to Accelerate Progress in Improving Maternal and Child Nutrition?" *The Lancet* 382: 536–51.

SABER-ECD Policy and Program Instruments, Indonesia. 2014. World Bank.

SABER-ECD Policy Instruments, Indonesia 2014. World Bank.

Schady, N., C. Araujo, P. Carneiro, and Y. Cruz-Aguyao. 2014. "Is Kindergarten Too Late?" Presentation at Institute of Medicine Forum: Investing in Young Children Globally, April 2014, Washington, DC.

Schweinhart, L., J. J. Montie, Z. Xiang, W. S. Barnett, C. R. Belfield, and M. Nores. 2005. *Lifetime Effects: The High/Scope Perry Pre-school Study through Age 40.* Ypsilanti, MI: High/Scope Educational Research Foundation.

Seyfried, L. 2011. *Family Planning and Maternal Health: The Effects of Family Planning on Maternal Health in the Democratic Republic of Congo.* Washington, DC: Georgetown University.

Spears, D. 2013. "How Much International Variation in Child Height Can Sanitation Explain?" Policy Research Working Paper No. 6351, World Bank, Washington, DC.

UNESCO. 2014. *Early Childhood Care and Education: Addressing Quality in Formal Pre-primary Learning Environments.* Paris: UNESCO.

Unesco-Orealc. 2004. "Intersectoral Co-ordination in Early Childhood Policies and Programmes: A Synthesis of Experiences in Latin America." Regional Bureau of Education for Latin America and the Caribbean, United National Educational, Scientific and Cultural Organization.

UNESCO-OREALC. 2004. "Intersectoral Co-ordination in Early Childhood Policies and Programmes: A Synthesis of Experiences in Latin America." Regional Bureau of Education for Latin America and the Caribbean, UNESCO.

UNICEF. 2009. *The State of the World's Children—Maternal and Newborn Health.* New York: UNICEF.

———. 2012. *Inequities in Early Childhood Development: What the Data Say. Evidence from the Multiple Indicator Cluster Surveys.* New York UNICEF.

Valerio, A., and M. Garcia. 2012. "Effective Financing." In *Handbook of Early Childhood Development Research and Its Impact on Global Policy*, edited by P. Britto, P. L. Engle, and C. M. Super, S2013. New York: Oxford University Press.

Vargas-Barón, E. 2005. *Planning Policies for Early Childhood Development: Guidelines for Action.* Paris: UNESCO/ADEA/UNICEF (United Nations Educational, Scientific and Cultural Organization/Association for the Development of Education in Africa/ United Nations Children's Fund).

Victoria, B. H., L. Adair, C. Fall, P. C. Hallal, R. Martorell, L. Richter, and H. S. Sachdev. 2008. "Maternal and Child Undernutrition: Consequences for Adult Health and Human Capital." *The Lancet* 371 (9609): 340–57.

Walker, S. P., T. D. Wachs, S. Grantham-McGregor, N. N. Black, C. A. Nelson, S. L. Huffman, H. Baker-Henningham, S. M. Chang, J. D. Hamadani, B. Lozoff, J. M. Meeks-Gardner, A. Powell Cam Rahman, and L. Richter. 2011. "Inequality in Early Childhood: Risk and Protective Factors for Early Child Development." *The Lancet* 378: 1325–38.

WHO. 2014. *Family Planning.* World Health Organization: Geneva.

World Bank. 2010. *Stepping Up Skills for More Jobs and Higher Productivity.* Washington, DC: World Bank.

———. 2013. *Spending More or Spending Better: Improving Education Financing in Indonesia.* Education Public Expenditure Review. Jakarta: World Bank. Based on Law 20/2003, King et al. (2004) and PP 38/2007.

———. 2014. Chapter 6: Early Childhood Education and Development in "Republic of Indonesia Medium Term Development Plan Support: A Compilation of Chapters Provided for the Background Study for Indonesia's Medium Term Development Plan (2015–2019)." Report No: AUS8490.

Young, M. E., ed. 2002. *From Early Child Development to Human Development.* Washington, DC: World Bank.

Zwane, A. P., and M. Kremer. 2007. "What Works in Fighting Diarrheal Diseases in Developing Countries? A Critical Review." *World Bank Research Observer* 22 (1): 1–24.

Environmental Benefits Statement

The World Bank Group is committed to reducing its environmental footprint. In support of this commitment, the Publishing and Knowledge Division leverages electronic publishing options and print-on-demand technology, which is located in regional hubs worldwide. Together, these initiatives enable print runs to be lowered and shipping distances decreased, resulting in reduced paper consumption, chemical use, greenhouse gas emissions, and waste.

The Publishing and Knowledge Division follows the recommended standards for paper use set by the Green Press Initiative. The majority of our books are printed on Forest Stewardship Council (FSC)–certified paper, with nearly all containing 50–100 percent recycled content. The recycled fiber in our book paper is either unbleached or bleached using totally chlorine free (TCF), processed chlorine free (PCF), or enhanced elemental chlorine free (EECF) processes.

More information about the Bank's environmental philosophy can be found at http://crinfo.worldbank.org/wbcrinfo/node/4.